PROBLEMS OF
AMERICAN FOREIGN POLICY

The Insight Series:

Studies in Contemporary Issues

from The Glencoe Press

Problems of American Foreign Policy
Martin B. Hickman

The Oppenheimer Affair:
A Political Play in Three Acts
Joseph Boskin and Fred Krinsky

The Politics of Religion in America
Fred Krinsky

The Welfare State:
Who is My Brother's Keeper?
Fred Krinsky and Joseph Boskin

Opposition Politics:
The Anti–New Deal Tradition
Joseph Boskin

Is American Democracy Exportable?
Edward G. McGrath

Protest from the Right
Robert A. Rosenstone

Democracy and Complexity:
Who Governs the Governors?
Fred Krinsky

Ferment in Labor
Jerome Wolf

Series Editors: Fred Krinsky and Joseph Boskin

PROBLEMS OF AMERICAN FOREIGN POLICY

Martin B. Hickman

Professor
Department of Political Science
Brigham Young University

THE GLENCOE PRESS
A Division of The Macmillan Company
Beverly Hills

Preface

The central purpose of this book is to bring together some carefully selected readings, which identify and explore the major problems in making foreign policy. Selection of these readings posed two major problems: first, how to provide an underlying unity to material taken from so many different authors and sources, and written for so many different purposes; second, how to avoid oversimplification of the foreign-policy process in an effort to present the "big picture." Whatever unity exists was obtained by concentrating on a limited number of interrelated themes: the nature of the foreign policy, the impact of our constitutional system on the policy process, the roles of the President and Congress, the reorganization of the State Department into an effective unit, and, lastly, the integration of military, intelligence, and diplomatic agencies into a single policy process. These themes are central to the problems of making foreign policy, but at the same time they provide a variety of viewpoints from which to examine the policy process.

Unity is preserved in yet another way. The themes emphasized in the readings have a natural cohesion not only because their subject matter is interrelated but also because they link the past to the present. Discussion of the foreign-policy process has focused on these themes for the past twenty years, and American involvement in Vietnam has renewed and sharpened this continuing concern. The current debate is centered on congressional-executive relations, but it has included all of the major issues raised in the readings. Moreover, participants in the debate are challenging concepts that have become accepted as basic truths. The most important of the concepts thus questioned is the notion that the President needs maximum freedom in conducting foreign policy. Opponents of American policy in Vietnam, many of whom espoused the concept of executive freedom in foreign policy, are now arguing that Congress must reassert its constitutional prerogative to check and supervise foreign policy. Hence the issues raised by the readings are particularly timely. Indeed, perhaps at no time in American history have students of the foreign-policy process had a better opportunity to subject the accepted truths about making foreign policy to the searching test of experience.

To concentrate on a few major themes could lead to dangerous oversimplification. Some of my friends in the State Department doubt whether it is possible to reduce the complexities of the foreign-policy process to understandable patterns without robbing the description of all meaning. These people are struck by how often policy is determined by chance, caprice and personality conflicts. Unless the student sees such forces at work, they argue, he will never fully understand the way foreign policy is made. I recognize the legitimacy of their fears without fully sharing them. Decision making is necessarily a dynamic process, difficult to describe in full detail. When asked to reconstruct the process, even decision makers themselves are apt to "tidy up" the thoughts and connections that led to action. The task of the analyst or observer is to see if there are underlying patterns beneath the apparent confusion. Moreover, the grasp of these patterns is often more important to an understanding of the decision-making process than the details, since these patterns give the details their full meaning.

Without some central organizing concepts, students will mistake the confusion and caprice, so easy to identify in the policy process, as the whole of reality. The readings in this book present, for the most part, the organizing concepts and tend, therefore, to obscure the complexity of the foreign-policy process; they were selected in full recognition of this limitation. I hoped that the student provided with a conceptual framework would be better prepared to see the details of the policy process in their proper perspective. The learning process is in essence the task of applying general concepts to specific situations and thereby discovering not only the limitations of the generalizations, but also how they can be reformulated to improve their usefulness. The organizing concepts found in this collection of readings are, therefore, not the final word but a useful starting point.

I would be less than grateful if I did not take this opportunity to thank those who helped in the preparation of this book. Professor Fred Krinsky, Chairman of the Political Science Department of the University of Southern California, gave his full support to the project and held me to my task when I would have put it aside. My research assistant, Martin Omansky was relentless in his pursuit of detail and bore gracefully the many burdens I laid on him.

Martin B. Hickman

Provo, Utah
November, 1967

Contents

PROBLEMS OF
AMERICAN FOREIGN POLICY

Chapter One

Thinking about Foreign Policy

The making of American foreign policy is beset with difficulties. In the first place, no one has yet been able to answer satisfactorily the question: What is foreign policy? The traditional answer has been that foreign policy is the official acts of the government in relation to other countries. But this definition has been challenged, for it has become increasingly clear that a freedom march in Alabama, or the refusal to serve an African diplomat at a drive-in in Maryland, or teach-ins at American universities all affect the making and conduct of foreign policy. Is the presence of an American oil company in the Middle East a question of concern to American foreign policy? If so, then what about an American shirt manufacturer in Hong Kong? The mere posing of these questions shows that the simple answers of thirty or even twenty years ago no longer suffice.

Another source of confusion is the truism that, in the United States, foreign policy is ultimately made by the President. To know this tells little about the way in which the President obtains the information and advice on which foreign policy is based. If one looks at a chart showing the organization of the United States government, it is obvious that the Secretary of State and the Department of State advise the President on matters of foreign policy. But experience since World War II has taught us that the organizational units to which the President turns for advice and information vary from situation to situation. The easy answer, then, that the Secretary of State is the President's adviser on questions of foreign policy conceals the growing importance of the Secretary of Defense and of the Presidential Assistant for National Security Affairs, both of whom are playing more and more important roles in making foreign policy. Unless we look beyond the Department of State to the

Department of Defense, to the Central Intelligence Agency, to the Department of Commerce, to the Treasury Department, and to the fifty-odd departments and agencies with foreign policy interests, we will not see the whole picture. Furthermore, we must look beyond the governmental officials to those public and private citizens who have the President's ear, if we are to find the threads of influence out of which the President eventually weaves the policy fabric.

Finally, there is the relation of the internal structure of the nation to the making of foreign policy. Clearly, internal situations influence foreign policy. The strength or weakness of political groups in the country will make one policy feasible and condemn another. Great Britain's need to trade in order to live has a profound influence on the kind of foreign policy it adopts. A balance-of-payments problem in the United States forces the policy-maker to determine whether military and foreign economic aid is worth the cost. The military power of the Soviet Union permits it to undertake one kind of foreign policy, the military weakness of Belgium dictates another. Although there is much dispute about the precise nature of the relationship, certainly ideology affects foreign policy. Economic growth and political stability are also related to foreign policy.

While it is generally recognized that these internal factors influence the content of foreign policy, it is not always clear that the same is true of the way in which governments are organized and operated.

The Constitution of the United States divides and separates government powers in a complex pattern. This division of power — federalism and separation of powers — has had a significant impact on our internal political life. Federalism has not directly affected the formulation and conduct of foreign policy, for the Constitution assigns full power over this phase of the nation's life to the federal government. Separation of powers is, however, a fact of political life that has profoundly influenced the making of foreign policy. Indeed, an examination of the implications of this division of power preoccupies most analysts of the foreign policy process in the United States.

The readings in this section, and the questions that follow each reading, have been selected to raise issues surrounding these problems. The first selection, "The Distinctive Environment of Foreign Policy" by Martin B. Hickman, provides intellectual scaffolding. The article emphasizes the difference between the environments of foreign and of domestic policy. It also assesses the impact of this difference on the foreign policy process and on the national interest as a guide to foreign policy.

The paper by Charles A. McClelland, entitled "Many American Foreign Policies," is a sharp reminder that first one must see the fragmented nature of the foreign policy process; then, one can understand the implications of this fragmentation for the formulation of foreign policy. McClelland's use of the word "game" does not mean that he thinks foreign policy matters are trivial. On the contrary, his purpose is the important one of alerting the reader to the fact that the subject matter and players in the foreign policy game are constantly shifting and changing.

The third selection, "The Constitutional Setting of Policy," by Paul Seabury, shows that the relations between the internal structure of a nation and its foreign policy are profound. Our government's internal nature exerts more than a temporary influence in solving a current problem; it reaches into the very heart of our democratic society and underlies all our relationships throughout the world.

The Distinctive Environment of Foreign Policy

Martin B. Hickman

In matters of foreign policy, most Americans know what they would do if they were the President and confidently expect that fidelity to principles and application of common sense will yield the right answers. The serious student of the foreign policy process must look beyond the generalities of "conventional wisdom" for a guide to understanding foreign policy. At the beginning, he must grasp the simple yet decisive difference between the environment in which *domestic policy* is carried out and that in which *foreign policy* operates. He should see that, while these environments are similar because their components are the same, they are also different because these components function in sharply different ways. He must understand that, because the environments are different, guides to successful foreign policy are often ambiguous, and that the foreign policy process is frequently hampered by the absence of information and by the pressure of time. In the course of this paper we shall examine each of these problems.

A comparison of the domestic and of the foreign policy environments must focus on the interaction among three components — norms, interests, and force — for these interactions determine the nature of the environment. But before examining these relationships, it is necessary to define with some care each component. (1) Norms are values shared by the individuals or groups in the environment. These values are expressed as legal norms, which we call laws, or as ideas about the way individuals and groups ought to behave in society, which we call ethical, moral, or social norms. The primary distinction between legal and other norms rests on the way they are enforced. Legal norms are generally enforced by the political community, while other norms are enforced through the pressure of family, peer groups, or public opinion. (2) Interests are goals that individuals or groups believe are necessary to their existence, prosperity, or prestige. In the domestic environment, the groups may be business, social, professional, labor, or religious; in the international environment, interest groups are primarily nations. (3) Force is the use of coercive measures to obtain compliance with a legal norm when voluntary compliance is not forthcoming. It is also used to realize an interest.

The Domestic Environment

In the domestic environment, law is the fundamental determinant wherever conflict arises between interests and law. The conflict is ordinarily resolved in favor of law. Ownership of property, for example, is determined by which party satisfies the legal norms governing the ownership and transfer of property. Neither the interests of the parties nor the ability of one party to physically coerce the other is relevant to the question of ownership. Enforcement of law is the responsibility of a central decision-maker who can use the full power of the community to ensure compliance.

Although legal norms are pre-eminent in the domestic environment, interests are also important. Indeed, the competition among various interests on the domestic scene constitutes what we call politics. Interests cannot be realized unless they are transformed into norms through the legislative process. Where individuals or groups seek to impose their interests on others without transforming them into legal norms the power of the community is interposed. This means that, at least in a democracy, interests cannot become norms until a substantial number of individuals or groups are prepared to accept them as the common interest and, therefore, binding on the whole community. This process is clearly seen in the attempt to prohibit the making, selling, and transporting of alcoholic beverages in the United States. In the early 1920's, a substantial pressure group was successful in convincing the majority of the nation that prohibition was really the common interest. The Eighteenth Amendment was adopted, transforming the interest of this pressure group into the legal norm for the nation. Prohibition went from a legal norm to an interest when opponents of prohibition were successful in obtaining the repeal of the Eighteenth Amendment in 1933.

In the domestic environment, the right to use force is limited to a central authority, government, in accordance with the legal norms of the community. Force is used to enforce legal norms, to maintain internal law and order, and to protect the community from external enemies. Those who encroach on the government's right to use force are labeled criminals and punished. Only when people are willing to obey the laws can force be used effectively, because the potential effectiveness of force depends significantly on the extent to which it does not have to be used. In the domestic environment, compliance can be relied on because a majority of citizens prefer their own country over all other political units, both internal and external, which compete for their loyalty.

International Environment

In the international environment, unlike the domestic environment, the legal norm, i.e. international law, does not ultimately determine behavior. International law does exist, it is true, but each nation in the international community retains full power to determine the extent of its own responsibility under international law, unless the nation has specifically delegated its power to an international organization. This decentralization introduces an element of caprice into international law, for there is no final arbiter of its meaning. A nation, therefore, cannot assume that its interpretation of international law will coincide with the interpretation made by other nations. Consequently, although nations may prefer to comply with international law as they see it, they realize that different interpretations by other nations may well jeopardize their most vital interests.

This decentralization gives the relationship between norms and interests in the foreign environment an entirely different character from that in the domestic environment. Whereas in the domestic environment norms regulate and control interests, ordinate and competitive guides to action. The dictates of in-in the international environment norms and interests are co-terests and of international law are frequently compatible and, when this is so, policy making is relatively easy. Where they are incompatible, making foreign policy is more difficult; then, the merits of these competitive guides must be weighed. In the past, the tendency has been for nations to follow national interests rather than international law, whenever their power has been sufficient to make this decision feasible. Of course, nations advance an interpretation of international law that justifies their behavior, but, as we have seen, each country decides for itself how to apply international law. The situation is fundamentally different from that of the domestic environment where the interpretation and enforcement of the law is in the hands of the central government.

In the international environment, the right to use force is not concentrated in a single authority, but is retained by each nation. International law provides that nations may legitimately use force in certain circumstances, the most familiar of which is self-defense. However, self-defense may be used by a nation to justify almost any action. In 1939, World War II began when Hitler asserted that Poland had attacked Germany and that Germany's counterattack was clearly self-defense. In 1967, after the outbreak of hostilities between Egypt and Israel, both countries charged the other with aggression; each was sure that their own use of force was justified by their right of self-defense under international law. It is clear then that as long as the power to interpret international law is not given to a central authority, each country is free to decide whether to use force for the maintenance of international law and order or for the advancement of its own interests. Each nation also decides whether it will take action unilaterally or in cooperation with other nations through international organizations such as the Organization of American States, the North Atlantic Treaty Organization, or the United Nations.

Because international law and national interests are coordinate and competing standards of behavior in the international environment, ever present is the possibility that a nation will use force either to obtain its version of international law or to assure the realization of its national interests. Stanley Hoffmann has pointed out that, while "procedures for cooperation, for the creation and expression of consent, exist in both domestic and world politics, the permanent possibility of free and legitimate recourse to violence remains the mark of international relations." [1]

In recapitulation, then, we see that domestic policy operates in an environment where legal norms receive substantial compliance or are systematically enforced where necessary. Interests exist but are not controlling, unless they become transformed into norms by the legislative process. Force is controlled by a central authority which possesses a legitimate monopoly over its use. On the other hand, foreign policy operates in an arena where legal norms are not controlling, where national interests may be used to justify violation of the legal norms, and where no central authority has the monopoly over the use of force.

Guides to Policy

It has been frequently asserted that, in the international environment described above, a healthy concern for the national interest is the cornerstone of a successful foreign policy. Hans Morgenthau and George Kennan assert that this concern has been absent in the making of American foreign policy. American policy-makers, they allege, have mistakenly supposed that the moral and legal values on the domestic scene prevail to the same extent in the international arena. This "moral-legalistic" ap-

---

[1] In *The State of War* (New York: Frederick A. Praeger, Inc., 1965), p. 89.

proach, they say, has obscured the national interest and has led the United States into questionable policies during the past half-century. These critics argue that the national interest must be the basis of any rational policy in a world where there is no central authority and where there are deep-rooted disputes over the existence and meaning of common norms.

There is, of course, a good deal of justice in this criticism. However, it raises a number of questions which must be answered before the criticism can be assessed. First, what is the national interest? This term has as many meanings as there are people who use it. In an attempt to make the concept a guide to policy-makers, it has been redefined as "national security." But this redefinition is not without a certain ambiguity of its own. Some military leaders and their supporters believe that national security can be achieved only when a nation is sufficiently strong to cope with any possible military threat. As has been often noted, such efforts in the past generally have been interpreted by other nations as creating new threats to their own security, and they have countered by increasing armaments. This reaction has spurred the first nation to redouble its own efforts, and an arms race, accompanied by an increased possibility of armed conflict, has resulted. Other policy-makers believe that national security is more likely to be won when all nations voluntarily comply with international law, that a rational foreign policy should rely more heavily on the rule of law than on military might. It must be clear, therefore, that national interest, defined as national security, is not an infallible guide to policy-making but rather an all-encompassing goal which leaves the question of means open.

One cannot escape the conclusion that neither the national interest nor international law can alone provide a sure guide to foreign policy. Just as reliance on legal norms in international affairs without regard for interest can lead to unrealistic foreign policies, so reliance on interest to the exclusion of international law leads to an increase in conflict among nations; the scales become heavily weighted on the side of the strong and cynical, which in turn, as we have noted, leads to an increase in the instability of the international system. It becomes necessary, then, to judge the relevance of each of these components in a given historical situation. There are no hard-and-fast rules to assure

the success of this effort. But recognition that foreign and domestic policies exist in substantially different environments, permits sounder conceptualization than does the assumption that the
two environments are the same.

The Policy Process

The first step in understanding foreign policy is to grasp the
basic distinction between the domestic and the foreign environments; the second is to see how this difference influences the policy
process.

The integrated relationship of norms, interests, and force
in the *domestic* environment provides the policy-maker with a
substantial degree of control over the environment. As a consequence, the policy process is essentially legislative and is characterized by investigation, discussion, and careful weighing of
the evidence. In most cases there is sufficient time for exhaustive
hearings, where competing interests have their day in court, and
there is also sufficient time for extensive debate of the relative
merits of these interests. Clearly, domestic policy-makers do not
have perfect information and unlimited time. If they did, the
whole task could be assigned to a computer complex. But time
pressure and lack of information are not the principal problems
that confront domestic policy-makers; their crucial concerns are
determining the meaning of the evidence and deciding among
competing interests. Since this task cannot be performed without
adequate information and sufficient time, the tendency in making
domestic policy is to delay decisions until the necessary information is at hand and until time has been taken to consider that
information.

The nonintegrated relationship of norms, interests, and force
in the international environment deprives the *foreign* policy
maker of substantial control over the environment. Foreign policy
frequently has to be made on the basis of inadequate information
and under severe time pressure. Consequently, the policy process
is executive in nature. The decision-maker must be given authority
to handle information as he sees fit, including the right to conceal
information from potential external enemies and from citizens of
his own nation. The foreign policy-maker also needs wide discretion because he must reach decisions rapidly. It is important,

then, to examine closely how the lack of information and the lack of time affect the foreign policy process.

Foreign policy often has to be made in the absence of all the relevant information. What was the intention of the USSR in placing missiles in Cuba in 1962? Was this move meant to upset the existing power relationship in the Carribean, or did the Soviets really believe these missiles to be defensive weapons against an attack from the United States? What would be the Russian reaction to a blockade, to an air strike, or to an invasion? Although definitive answers to these questions were not at hand, a decision would have been made with greater certainty had more reliable information been available.

In the international environment, information is often inadequate for a number of reasons, but the following are particularly important: (1) In each country, the foreign policy makers do everything they can to conceal the extent of their information from the policy-makers of other countries. Indeed, most nations have elaborate security systems to protect classified information and complicated codes to assure this secrecy during transmission. Conversely, nations expend considerable time, money, and manpower to penetrate other nations' security systems. (2) Information may be fragmented, and it requires a good deal of effort to piece the puzzle together. Thus, most of the Central Intelligence Agency staff is assigned to the difficult and time-consuming task of putting together overt but fragmented information about the rest of the world. (3) Obviously, all the information available cannot be processed by the policy-maker. The important information must be separated from the unimportant, the reliable from the unreliable, and the relevant from the irrelevant before the policy-maker sees it. But this selection and sifting process may operate to hide information from the policy-maker rather than bring it to his attention. The Bay of Pigs [2] is perhaps the most recent case where a President has had cause to com-

---

[2] On April 17, 1961, a landing force of 1400 anti-Castro Cuban exiles, organized, financed, trained, and directed by the United States Central Intelligence Agency, was crushed in less than three days by superior numbers of Castro's army. Defeat was blamed on the fact that the CIA underestimated Cuba's military strength, did not coordinate its plans with the United States Department of Defense, and misjudged the extent of the support that the Cuban people were prepared to give the invasion.

plain about the selection process; Pearl Harbor is perhaps the most dramatic. (4) Closely related to the selection problem is that of conceptualization. There is a popular belief that the facts have one and only one meaning readily apparent to all observers. "Let the facts speak," we are fond of saying. The truth is, of course, that facts generally have meaning only within the conceptual framework the observer brings to the problem. There is no dispute about the fact of the American Civil War, but the meaning of that fact is still being debated long after its close. At Pearl Harbor, our intelligence system produced more than sufficient information in terms of quantity but failed to provide answers to pressing questions because the interpreters of that information brought a faulty conceptual framework to their task. Nor is there any dispute about the fact that, at the Munich conference of 1938, European leaders sacrificed Czechoslovakia to Hitler's territorial demands. In retrospect, this sacrifice represents the folly of appeasement; in 1938, to Sir Neville Chamberlain, British Prime Minister, it meant "peace in our time."

The possibility of error in the information process is rather large, and foreign policy makers must constantly be on the alert that both the factual data and the conceptualizations they bring to the study of that data are relevant to the problem to be solved. In the study of foreign policy making, it is apparent to the historian or critic that, in most cases where errors have been made, sufficient information was at hand to solve the problem if only it had been seen in the proper perspective. The essential problem, then, is not the raw data, although this must be a central concern of the information process. It is the continued re-evaluation of the conceptualizations the policy-maker brings to the problem at hand.

The problem of adequate information cannot be separated from the second variable we are considering — time. If time were not in short supply, the problem of gathering and analyzing information would be substantially easier. But foreign policy makers are constantly bedeviled by time pressures; decisions often cannot be postponed. The reasons for this constant time pressure are not always made explicit, and therefore it is worthwhile to examine three general situations in which time is an acute factor for foreign policy makers.

The first occurs when there is a reduction in the absolute time within which a decision must be reached. The most common example occurs when one nation presents another with an ultimatum that must be answered by a given date. The fixing of a specific termination point on the decision-making process forces a reduction in the number of alternatives considered and the extent to which each can be analyzed.

A second situation arises in crises characterized by a sharp increase in the number and variety of transactions between the parties to the dispute. Indeed, the interactions can occur so rapidly that the decision-maker becomes confused about the sequence. There is some evidence that the key to the solution to the Cuban missile crisis was the decision by the United States' policy-makers that Khrushchev's letters to President Kennedy were written in inverse order from their receipt.[3] This sudden increase in transactions means that, although there is no specific time limit placed on the decision-making process, the amount of time allowed for each decision must be reduced, for time is not an infinite resource. Moreover, the fact that the decision-making process is open-ended does not mean that the making of the decision can be postponed indefinitely. The flow of time forces changes in the alternatives open to the decision-maker; if he wishes to retain some options, he must move rapidly. In the Cuban missile crisis, the need to act before the missiles became operational was necessary if some desirable alternatives were to be kept open.

A third situation occurs when the problems are complex. The amount of time available for the decision may, in absolute terms, be relatively long, but, in terms of the problems facing the de-

---

[3] Two messages were received by the President. The first, dated Friday October 26, was a personal letter from Chairman Khrushchev proposing a generally acceptable outline for the resolution of the crisis. The second was broadcast on Saturday morning, the 27th. Its style suggested the handiwork of the Soviet Foreign Office, and it contained terms unacceptable to the President. Attorney General Kennedy suggested that the Saturday message be ignored — that the President should respond only to the October 26 letter. The President accepted this advice and communicated with the Chairman on the basis of the proposals in the Friday message. This tactic proved to be successful. It was later determined that the Saturday message was written before the Khrushchev letter, but, due to delays in the Soviet Foreign Office, was broadcast after the Friday letter had been received.

cision-maker, the absolute time may be relatively short. The acute crisis usually involves critical but fairly simple questions. The threat tends to be straightforward rather than ambivalent, the dangers clearly outlined, and the range of decision alternatives limited. President Truman's decision to use American forces in Korea in 1950 illustrates this type of situation. The problem of emerging Chinese power exemplifies a situation in which the issues are so complex that no guess can be made as to what would be a reasonable length of time in which to reach a decision. Frequently, such situations are called permanent crises to underline the fact that the amount of time in which to solve the problem will always be in short supply.

Insufficient time, inadequate information, and the ever-present possibility that nations will resort to the use of force profoundly influence the environment in which foreign policy is made. The result is that foreign policy makers must reach decisions in a much more uncertain environment than that in which domestic policymakers, operate. In reaching decisions about domestic policy, Americans have at least the great fundamentals of the Constitution to guide them. In making foreign policy, the environment provides only the signposts of international law and national interests, where ambiguities are as likely to confuse the decision-maker as to guide him. So formidable, therefore, are the problems of foreign policy makers that one would like to name irony and pity as their judges. But this cannot be; more trenchant performance standards must be imposed where questions of foreign policy are involved. As President Kennedy told his aides after the Bay of Pigs, "Domestic policy can only defeat us; foreign policy can kill us."

Questions

1. How does Professor Hickman distinguish between the domestic and the international environment? What are the characteristics of each, and how do they differ?
2. "Enforcement of norms in the international environment is difficult because of conflicting national interests." Is "national interest" the only determinant of differences in perceptions of international law?
3. Discuss the time factor in domestic and international policy-making.
4. What is a "permanent crisis"?
5. "If only the President and the Department of State would just use common sense, we would be a lot better off." Comment.

Many American Foreign Policies: The Stresses from Multiple Goals and Complex Administration*

Charles A. McClelland

Charles A. McClelland is the author of *Nuclear Weapons, Missiles, and the Future of War, The United Nations, the Continuing Debate,* and *Systems Theory in International Relations.* He is presently Professor of International Relations at the University of Southern California and was Director of the Center for Conflict Resolution at The University of Michigan in 1966 and 1967.

The formulation and execution of foreign policy have become such complex processes that it may be actually misleading to refer to U. S. foreign policy as if it were a single thing. A critic should always realize that an announced policy position will always be varied and even diluted when it is extended, in practice, through a large, human organization. It is well known that important elected officials, including the President of the United States, who have pledged that they would make sweeping changes in government are, in fact, hemmed in and intricately contained by the permanent structures of government organization. It is extremely difficult to effect drastic changes in any big bureaucracy. Whether it is public or private appears to make little difference. Compounding this problem is the diverse character of foreign policy activities. So many different purposes are being served; so many aims are being pursued; so many people are active in different organizations; and so monumental are the problems of overall coordination and control, that the notion of *a* foreign policy seems

*Abstracted in the Proceedings of the Institute of World Affairs, Fortieth Session 1963 "The Grand Design." Copyright 1964 by the University of Southern California, pp. 63-64. Professor McClelland granted permission to reprint his paper here in this form in July 1967.

to be quite inadequate. There is no one word, apparently, that describes the reality — no term by which one can refer to separate but concurrent activities that may be grouped by functional criteria, that are often overlapping in both conception and execution, and that are carried on according to differing rules of procedure and differing styles of action. We might refer to the multiples of foreign policy by calling them groups of games. This is acceptable, if we remove from the concept of a "game" the elements of artificiality or of contrived situations and if we eliminate the notion of terminal wins and losses. Such a general meaning appears to be conveyed in the vernacular expression, "What's your game?"

Each foreign policy "game" is carried along by its special community of civil servants and officials. For descriptive purposes, we can conceive of these games as having distinctive rules; each game is intended to serve the national interest in international relations in a special way. Each game can be characterized according to its main function and with respect to how its players expect to forward the general objectives of peace, safety, power, and prosperity for the United States....

The first of these games of foreign policy is the traditional one. The *diplomatic game* in which the Department of State plays the principal part involves the maintenance of official representation abroad, the gathering of data from other countries particularly having to do with the intentions, strategies, and capabilities of other governments in international politics, and the planning of specific foreign policies.

The *military game* is, of course, related to the diplomatic game but its basic object, between wars, is to anticipate, plan, and prepare for all possible armed conflicts in which the country may become involved. Since World War II, the American military establishment has lost much of its peacetime passivity and innocence which have been traditional. Instead, it has become deeply involved in a hybrid military-political-technological game that goes by the title of "national security affairs."

A third game of foreign policy is played by the intelligence community. The objectives of the *intelligence game* are to gather, organize, and analyze the information of international affairs and, in some circumstances, to act in the field in matters that are regarded as highly sensitive, highly secret, or both. The intelligence function is a part of other games of foreign relations but, over the past 15 years, a superstructure of very considerable size and authority has been erected in the Central Intelligence Agency, the National Security Agency, and some other organizations. Much of the intelligence game is devoted to penetrating foreign intelligence organizations and to preventing infiltration by agents of other intelligence communities. All but the general nature of intelligence operations remains secret; it is said, however, that something on the order of 80% of the sources used in the work are open and public.

At the other end of the spectrum is the *information game*. Its function is to distribute in other publics large amounts of fact and opinion that are expected to create attitudes and images abroad that are favorable to the United States or that are to its advantage, in one way or another. It is a curious fact, not known widely among Americans, that the United States Information Agency whose work abroad is largely (and necessarily) public is restrained by law from reporting in any detail on what it does and how it operates in the international system.

A fifth game of foreign affairs involving both policy-making and actions in the field is concerned with fostering and promoting business opportunities abroad and with watching over changing conditions in the international trading system. Although the *international business game* is shared by several governmental departments including the Department of State, its home is in the Department of Commerce where an organization of respectable size directs the play.

Foreign assistance has blossomed into yet another game of foreign policy. In recent years, it has acquired a large role in the relations with underdeveloped countries of Asia, Africa, and Latin America. The *national development game* expands inevitably from restricted concerns with economic assistance to the wider fields of educational, cultural, and social development programs. The Agency for International Development (AID), as an organization in but not of the Department of State, exists to manifest the partially autonomous character of the development game. The Congress, in its scrutiny of the foreign assistance program, has, in effect, been calling into question the viability of the game, the effectiveness of its book of rules, and the cost/effectiveness ratio of the play.

Further, there is an identifiable *security game* the object of which is to prevent damage and loss to the nation in situations that range from fingerprinting visitors from other countries, to customs inspections, abating illegal entries into the country, keeping surveillance over possible subversive activities, to guarding secret documents and "clearing" persons for work with classified materials. Although the Federal Bureau of Investigation does a part of this work, there are numerous government offices that are engaged in one or several of the aspects of the very specialized security game.

Although it is important to stress that efforts are made constantly to coordinate all these special functions, or foreign policy games, as we have called them, there are real differences in the outlooks, emphases, and preferred methods of work of the participants in each of the games. The incredibly difficult task of balancing the different games in an effective "mix" falls to both the executive and legislative branches of government; it is a national problem of prime importance. Because organizations quickly adopt distinctive operational codes and institutionalize their practices, disagreements and tensions develop in interagency relations; it becomes the conviction of each and every agency that it is second to none in its devotion to national objectives in international relations. While this is normal, it obstructs the adjustment of the "mix." Yet, in a shifting international environment that has different characteristics in different parts of the world, the ability to change the games and to adjust the weights of different foreign policy games has the closest possible relationship to the execution of a successful foreign policy. The expert manipulation of the "mix" of foreign policy is a skill that we have yet to achieve in full measure. The fault lies as much in the active public as in the government.

If the responsible and concerned citizen is to understand American foreign policy, he needs more than a constantly refreshed source of specific information about how policy is carried into practice abroad. In addition, he needs to realize that there are various non-identical foreign policy games being carried on concurrently by different men in different organizations working in behalf of a number of secondary objectives. The Department of Commerce exists to assist buying and selling at home and abroad and when it undertakes to negotiate the sale of wheat surpluses to Communist customers, it would be surprising, indeed, if there were no reservations among some of those who are engrossed in the actions of the military and diplomatic games. Many of the proposed moves that make sense in the playing of the diplomatic game appear to be risky to an unnecessary degree in the perspective of the intelligence community. Some citizen awareness of natural differences in outlook and some understanding of the requirements of the specialized games would contribute to the growth of sophistication in American foreign relations. We should realize that most of this is a new development. If the Department of State, which a good many citizens seem to distrust as *the* fountainhead of all foreign policy, good and bad alike, were suddenly removed from the scene, there would still remain a very substantial foreign policy machinery of great size, extent, and importance — more extensive in every way, in fact, than the whole of the Department of State as it was in 1941.

. . . .

If we wish to think in terms of American foreign policy as a single, whole phenomenon, then we must, at least, recognize its present complexity and apply our evaluations according to its numerous aspects. We should judge in terms of a number of different instruments of policy and of a range of immediate objectives, not all of which are perfectly compatible, one with another. . . .

Questions

1. What internal bureaucratic factors limit the President's ability to change the foreign policy of the United States? Do you believe that these limitations are desirable?
2. In what sense does Professor McClelland use the word "game"?
3. Is it not true that concocting a policy "mix" is only an exercise in educated guesswork or intuition? How can Professor McClelland be so specific when the subject matter is so vague?
4. Charles A. Lindbergh's flight to Paris affected United States - French

relations. Grace Kelly's marriage to Prince Ranier of Monaco touched the hearts of millions of romantic Europeans. Are these incidents, in reality, factors in foreign policy? Do they require another "game"/or would you unsympathetically attach them to the "international business game," Bureau of Tourism?

The Constitutional Setting of Policy*

Paul Seabury

Paul Seabury is Associate Professor of Political Science at the University of California at Berkeley and the author of *The Wilhelmstrasse, A Study of German Diplomats under the Nazi Regime* and *The Waning of Southern Internationalism.* He has been chairman of the executive committee of Americans for Democratic Action, Visiting Fellow at the Center for International Studies at Princeton University, Resident Professor at the Brookings Institution, and a Guggenheim Fellow.

Order is the first desideratum for the simple reason that chaos means non-existence. — REINHOLD NIEBUHR.

In the past twenty years, organizational innovations to cope with international crisis have profoundly affected all spheres of American government and policies. The kinds of public transactions occurring between the United States and other nations have grown. Traditional American diplomatic and military establishments have been enlarged beyond belief, and their tasks both diversified and intensified. Secret intelligence and propaganda have been added to them. The overseas activities of once domestic governmental agencies like the Departments of Labor, Agriculture, and Treasury have become global in scope. Requirements of speed, flexibility, and adaptability have greatly strained traditional modes of administration. New international organizations

---

*From *Power, Freedom and Diplomacy*, by Paul Seabury. © Copyright 1963 by Random House, Inc., New York City. Reprinted by permission.

add a further multilateral dimension to the encounters and transactions of states. Everything is related to everything else. This organizational revolution is hardly unique to the United States. But due to the central position of the United States in the non-Communist world, the making of American foreign policy, never an easy task, has been altered beyond belief.

The management of foreign affairs seems to many people an arcane and obscure affair. Not secrecy alone (a perpetual problem of democracies in foreign affairs), but also complexity, have made it virtually incomprehensible to the man in the street, and deeply puzzling at times even to many men who work within the labyrinthine corridors of government itself. American social scientists and journalists today attempt to light up these corridors by crystallizing or photographing the complex processes of decision-making. But they constantly run up against the extraordinary difficulty that the processes appear so ephemeral, and so contingent upon changing global political problems. The processes seemingly depend too upon constant shifts in locale and intensity of human power, vigor, lethargy, purpose, and resources. Representative government and democracy are based in theory upon the principle of consent of the governed and the accountability of government to society; but consent, accountability, and responsibility are often hard come by, in such times.

The Umbrella of Constitutional Order

We might first ask whether these processes take place under the larger umbrella of some established constitutional order. Today many states in the society of nations are, in a certain sense, *only* processes, so new, provisional, and transitory do their political institutions appear. Nearly a third of the total United Nations membership today consists of nation-states which did not exist ten years ago. But even many "older" state entities today appear equally provisional as far as their basic constitutional order and their claim to statehood is concerned. A governmental process which we see today may, like that of the United Arab Republic, simply not exist tomorrow. The legitimacy of a particular existing constitutional order may be widely challenged, both at home or abroad. In some states, there is not even a rudimentary popular consciousness of nationality, much less a popular acceptance of the existing constitutional order of things.[1] Such conditions provoke instability and indeterminacy in foreign affairs. Harold Lasswell's generally insufficient description of the State as a "manifold of events" [2] is quite appropriate for many of these valuable and volatile nations, notably those of the new Afro–Asian bloc, where tradition, custom, and a domestic political consensus are too rudimentary to amount to much.

A state or political community must have a stable constitutional order if it is to survive in the sea of events around it. Yet such an order, essential elements of which are popular consent and understanding, is present in the world today only among a few of the more highly integrated and historically deep-rooted political communities of the Western world. Clearly it exists in Great Britain and the United States. Their political orders are regarded as much more than ephemeral processes. They are widely comprehended, authoritative arrangements of political power. The state itself is subordinate to this constitutional order, which, so it is said, both legitimizes the exercise of political power and sets limits upon it. While one might point to some states in the Soviet or Communist world as also possessing rudimentary elements of popular consent and political continuity, it should be pointed out that force and violence play an essential role in their constitutional stability. Marxist theory about the state explicitly proclaims its provisional character: i.e., the state is an historically contingent entity which shall pass away when certain objective transformations have taken place in society. Marxist doctrine thus

---

[1] An extreme instance of this political condition may be seen today in the relationship of the West German *Bundesrepublik* and the Soviet *Deutsche Demokratische Republik* of East Germany. No one would deny the existence, in Germany as a whole, of something known as consciousness of nationality, but there is hardly any popular consensus about the desirable territorial or constitutional order of things. West German Foreign Minister von Brentano, when asked whether the *Bundesrepublik* would be willing to negotiate about the relationship of these two regimes, replied, "Yes, but not with the prison guards" (namely, the East German authorities). Washington *Post*, October 15, 1961.

[2] See his *Psychopathology and Politics*, rev. ed. New York: Viking, 1960, Ch. XIII. "The time-space abstraction of the 'group,' " Lasswell writes, "is just as 'real' or 'unreal' as the time-space abstraction called the 'individual.' They are both equally real or unreal, and they stand and fall together." This definition would be equally adequate and puzzling to both Queen Elizabeth and Mr. Moise Tshombe as descriptive of their respective states.

provisionalizes even the institutions of the Soviet world itself. . . .

A supreme constitutional problem of all national political entities is that of arranging both authority and political power so that the state may legitimately, purposively, and effectively act in the realm of world politics, a realm occupied by many other states similarly claiming their sovereign rights. In relatively stable political entities, the foreign policy processes thus possess a certain orderliness and stability. These foreign policy processes are products of a perpetual tension between constitutional forms and unique political contingencies of the moment.

A constitution is not merely a description of transitory allocations of political influence and power in a state; it is also something less than a description of the totality of form and order in the whole society. In Western political thought, a constitutional order signifies a government of laws, not of men. Ultimate authority theoretically resides in supreme law, with which lesser laws, enacted by men, supposedly should harmonize. A constitutional order is ideally an order in which political power is legitimized, allocated, limited, and synchronized. A constitutional order not merely legitimizes the exercise of political power but also serves to ensure its orderly, civil transfer so that there may be continuity of government among men. Two general types of politics might be distinguished here for our purposes: the political system which is constitutional by the above definition and the one which is not. For while all regimes and governments exercise political power by nature and customarily seek to perpetuate themselves, some are essentially formless or even limitless both in the power they seek, and the objects over which they would employ it.

A nonconstitutional political system could be defined as one in which the actual distribution of power differs radically from the proclaimed or specified distribution of power which a written document, basic law, or customary usage may speak of. (Of course a written constitution may actually serve to obscure the essential order of things.) But in the modern totalitarian state, a nonconstitutional order may have a certain formlessness of a political system which defies conceptualization because it contemptuously rejects restraints and forms. This quality has frequently been pointed out in Nazi totalitarianism. Not only did Hitler smash the

Weimar Constitution without even bothering to replace it with another "paper document" (something which the Bolsheviks, with their greater reverence for the State, did do quickly after seizing power); the very absence of any constitutional specification of rights and obligations, of distribution of powers, of any enduring perquisites and duties, or functional authorities meant that both in theory and fact the whole system was subject to change at any time. Thus, in a sense, there was no limit to power, since no form persisted. The concentration camps of Auschwitz, Belsen, and elsewhere are memorials to this condition. Attempts by Nazi constitutional apologists to legitimate the regime by proclaiming a direct, unmediated relationship between the Führer and the German Volk, whose will he supposedly expressed (just as Castro embodies the Cuban "will"), veiled a fatal constitutional flaw in the system which Hitler's defeat in war only further obscured: the system specified no legitimate procedure by which the charismatic leader's power and authority could be transmitted in orderly constitutional fashion to a successor. H. R. Trevor-Roper describes the Nazi political system as a court, but it was the court of a king, who, like the donkey, had neither pride of parentage nor hope of progeny.

A Juridical Contradiction

A curious juridical contradiction inheres in many Western constitutions, including that of the United States. While the domestic power of the state over its subjects is typically limited by the constitution (which specifies checks upon executive and lawmaking power) still, the power of the state in the larger context of the society of nations is invariably regarded as sovereign and plenary. Seen from the outside, the state is a juridical entity in international law, to be held accountable for its actions in the international society. It is also an entity which, charged with promoting the security and general welfare of its people, should act in a unitary fashion, even though its domestic, constitutional attributes of power may be juridically separated and divided. John Locke, one of the foremost political theorists of the English speaking world, sought to account for this necessary contradiction between the plenary sovereign power of the state and its executive in foreign affairs and the limited power of the constitutional state and executive power *within* the society. According to Locke:

> There is ... [a] power in every commonwealth which one may
> call natural, because it is that which answers to the power every
> man naturally had before he entered into society. For though in
> a commonwealth, the members of it are distinct persons, still in
> reference to one another, and as such are governed by the laws
> of the society; yet in reference to the rest of mankind, they
> make one body, which is, as every member of it before was,
> still in the state of nature with the rest of mankind, hence it
> is, that the controversies that happen between any man of the
> society with those that are out of it, are managed by the public;
> and an injury done to a member of their body engages the whole
> in the reparation of it. So that, under this consideration, the
> whole community is one body in the state of Nature, in respect
> of all other states or persons out of its community.

> This therefore contains the power of war and peace, leagues and
> alliances, and all the transactions, with all persons and commu-
> nities without the commonwealth; and may be called federative,
> if any one pleases. So the thing be understood, I am indifferent
> as to the name.

> These two powers, executive and federative, though they be
> really distinct in themselves, yet one comprehending the execu-
> tion of the municipal laws of the society within itself, upon all
> that are parts of it; the other the management of the security
> and interest of the public without, with all those that it may
> receive benefit or damage from; yet they are always almost
> united. And though this federative power in the well or ill man-
> agement of it be of great moment to the commonwealth, yet it
> is much less capable to be directed by antecedent, standing,
> positive laws than the executive; and so must necessarily be
> left to the prudence and wisdom of those whose hands it is in,
> to be managed for the public good. For the laws that concern
> subjects one amongst another, being to direct their actions,
> may well enough precede them. But what is to be done in
> reference to foreigners, depending much upon ... them, to be
> managed by the best of their skill, for the advantage of the
> commonwealth.[3]

---

[3] John Locke, *Of Civil Government*. New York: E. P. Dutton and Company, 1924, pp. 191–192.

Thus the domestic, executive authority of a constitutional commonwealth might be required to obey and to execute the laws made by a legislature and be subject to many constitutional restraints on his power. But in the realm of foreign affairs these legislative-executive functions became, in a sense, fused. To act swiftly, purposively in world politics to protect or advance the interests of the society itself, the federative power was thus liberated in significant ways from constitutional constraints. Locke sees an executive as a Janus: one head looking inward upon the constitutional society, benign and limited in its power and authority; the other, looking outward to the world, authoritative and powerful, speaking, acting, and legislating with the authority of the whole society itself. This Lockean distinction between federative and executive power is embodied in the United States Constitution.

The American Constitution and the Problem of Power

The Constitution and foreign policy can hardly be discussed without first pointing to the remarkable durability and adaptiveness of the American political framework. The Constitution is more than 170 years old, older than the written constitution of any other modern state. The unwritten British constitution may, of course, be regarded as a far older, though a far more elusive juridical order — an amalgam of customs, uses, prerogatives, statutes, and Acts of Parliament. In contrast, the constitution of the French Fifth Republic today is only four years old; and France, since 1789, has had more than seven written constitutions. But equally remarkable, the constitutional entities which the Constitution originally prescribed have persisted vigorously despite the massive changes in American society and culture since the eighteenth century. Most Americans take it for granted as the juridical framework within which political life occurs. All major movements in American political life, even those which have stood on the radical fringes of the political spectrum, have accepted the Constitution as a desirable, enduring framework of political power and discourse. Since the eighteenth century there has been no significant American political movement which explicitly rejected it or posed any constitutional alternative.

By way of contrast, in nineteenth and twentieth century

European politics, all of the major continental states have had profound disputes about what constitutional order was preferable. Thus, Professor Duverger, in writing of French politics, has made the interesting distinction between the "parties of order" and the "parties of movement," between those for whom a constitutional order was a paramount concern and those for whom political transformation was deemed superior to order itself. No such distinction could possibly be made in American politics, unless the American Communist Party were included in the argument. But even American Communists have recently been pressed into doctrinal conformity by denying un-Constitutional purposes! The great debate during the New Deal in the 1930's about the legitimacy of Roosevelt's social reforms was between those who denied their constitutionality and those who defended it. The great debate between North and South, preceding and during the Civil War, was couched also in constitutional terms, both sides stressing the correctness of their own constitutional interpretations. What was originally designed for thirteen states and four million people, chiefly farmers and craftsmen, now applies to a nation of fifty states and 180,000,000 people, living in a highly complex industrial society. Perhaps in no earlier period in history has a constitutional system ever shown such vigorous adaptability and staying power.

The Constitution has been a framework within which a political dialogue about domestic and foreign policy has taken place, but it also has been a powerful agent to "legitimately" organize, diffuse, and separate political power and rights. During international crises, when alternative American courses of action have been subjects of domestic political debate, the meaning of the Constitution has invariably been re-explored, particularly, as we shall see, with respect to the extent of interrelationships and limits of federal, Presidential, and Congressional powers. The chief purpose of the Constitution was to "establish a more perfect Union," but an ancillary purpose was to subject political power and to distribute it among disparate functional elements of the American body politic. In the *Federalist* papers, Madison justified this latter purpose: "We must not shut our eyes to the nature of man . . . All power in human hands is liable to be abused. No form of government can be a perfect guard against the abuse of power. The recommendation of the republican (form of government) is that the danger of abuse is less than in any other."

Skepticism about human nature and concern for human liberties and political order and prosperity thus established a continuing tension between the domestic constitutional order of a republican policy (with power distributed and separated) and the international needs of a sovereign state, which require a separate and more trenchant kind of authority. This tension has been enduring and necessary. As a consequence, the federative power necessary to the survival of a state has constantly endangered the organizational principles of a free society at all times.

Fear of possible abuse of centralized power runs like a thread through the history of American political thought. The dangers it poses to contemporary American freedoms were recently stressed by President Eisenhower in his Farewell Address to the American people in banuary 1961:

> In the councils of Government, we must guard against the acquisition of unwarranted influence, whether sought or unsought by the military-industrial complex. The potential for the disastrous rise of misplaced power exists and will persist.
>
> We must never let the weight of this combination endanger our liberties or democratic processes. We should take nothing for granted. Only an alert and knowledgeable citizenry can compel the proper meshing of the high industrial and military machinery of defense with our peaceful methods and goals, so that security and liberty may prosper together.[4]

This remarkable caveat against possible abuses of military power obscured from public attention at the time a warning by Eisenhower against another possible threat to individual liberties from quite another source: "In holding scientific research and discovery in respect, we must also be alert to the equal and opposite danger that public policy could itself become the captive of a scientific-technological elite."[5]

This fear was anticipated by the framers of the Constitution. Constitutional power was spatially and functionally dispersed:

---

[4] *The New York Times*, January 18, 1961.
[5] *Ibid.*

spatially, between a federal government and the governments of individual states; functionally, between executive, legislative, and judicial branches of government. The first ten amendments to the Constitution specify civil rights enjoyed by citizens against both federal and state authority. Within the overarching federal government, power was given in classic, Montesquieu fashion, to the President, the Congress, and the Supreme Court. The Bill of Rights, added to the Constitution as its first major amendment, specifies restraints upon the exercise of power by the state. It denies to authority, to government as a whole, certain powers which could conceivably make it limitless in power over the public and over individuals. Certain specified human rights of thought, expression, and action were juxtaposed to political authority, and the state, in theory, should not erode them. Freedom of speech, due process, free assembly, a free press — these provisions of the first ten amendments made explicit certain implicit characteristics of constitutions in general, i.e., the limitations upon state power *vis-à-vis* the public. Thus the authority of the American constitution came in part to consist of its own self-restraint and the restraints which it supposedly should instill in those who were to exercise legitimate authority in its name.

A tension developed between these doctrines of separation and limitation of powers and the exigencies of world politics. Domestic constitutionalism restrained power and established checks upon the modes and objects of its employment. A concern for national political and military security could often recommend exactly the opposite. In foreign affairs, protection of national interests and extension of American power abroad often seemed to require secrecy, authority, and almost authoritarian power. In conflicts of interest, ideology, or purpose among sovereign state entities, any state which was enfeebled by internal constitutional arrangements might be unable to act decisively. Such a state could not long endure and would inevitably fall victim, perhaps to its own domestic political virtues. Not without good reason did Tocqueville, in the early nineteenth century, write that democracies such as the United States seemed institutionally deficient in the realm of foreign affairs, incapable of pursuing any fixed design and perpetually inhibited by domestic political processes and whimsical wills of the public. What in a domestic context was virtue was in an international context a vice. Democracy, incapable of the purposefulness of authoritarian states, could be destroyed (or transformed into authoritarian form) by engaging in the necessary acts in which it was by nature least skillful. Logic, wisdom, and reason cannot dissipate insoluble political problems. The *Realpolitik* tendency was toward sharp centralization of state power for foreign policy purposes. The Constitutional tendency was to restore balance in politics and to assert the *separateness* of powers. During grave crises, the matter recurrently rose to the surface of American political discourse.

Some Constitutional lawyers thought this tension originated in deficiencies of the Constitution as a written document. Professor E. L. Corwin has described the Constitution as a "standing invitation to struggle for the privilege of directing American foreign policy." But the essential difficulty was not only what the Constitution (as written document) said, but what it did not or could not say, and finally, what the particular problems were which the founding fathers** probably preferred to evade by silence. The Constitution clearly specified basic, organizational forms and principles of the domestic polity, but its prescriptions for foreign affairs powers were brief, insufficient, and ambiguous. The difficulty was unavoidable: how to preserve the theory of separation and limitation of powers yet at the same time construct effective agencies of power, and authority, in dealing with other states.

We should not detract too much from the Constitution. It confirmed the supremacy of federal agencies and authorities over individual states in the management of foreign affairs; it vested the supreme and exclusive powers of treaty-making, war-making, and diplomacy in the federal government. Treaties were exclusively to be negotiated by the federal government. When ratified, they were to become the "supreme law of the land," thus,

---

**Eisenhower, during his benign reign, sometimes spoke of the Constitution and the Declaration of Independence as the "founding documents," an awkward yet intriguing remark which few Americans noted. It seemed to suggest that the "documents" had simply ordered the "founding fathers" to write them. The innocence of the remark reflects a widespread popular reverence, if not a mystique, which Americans have for these documents: if the Constitution did not exist, God would have had to invent it. On such strange, unfathomable premises do some stable constitutional orders persist.

presumably, prevailing over both state laws and prior Congressional legislation. States were enjoined from concluding treaties with other powers. Command over national armed forces was vested in the President as Commander-in-Chief. He could dispose of them as he saw fit. The power to declare a state of war was vested in the Congress, which itself was a creature of the federal government. By inference, so too did Congress come to possess the power to declare a state of war ended. The President, "by and with the advice and consent of the Senate," was empowered to negotiate and to conclude treaties. Finally, the President was empowered to "send and receive Ambassadors," a power subsequently interpreted to imply that he could also "not send," and "not receive," the essential power of recognition and non-recognition of foreign states.

Here ends the catalogue of "enumerated" powers over foreign affairs. Yet even when these scanty specifications were set alongside other constitutional provisions, potential institutional conflicts were obvious. Meager as the specifications were, they bore seeds of dissension. What was not said also proved ultimately more important than what was.

The enduring constitutional issue rested in a single problem. The United States was a sovereign state in a system of sovereign states. If such sovereign power were supreme, how much of it could constitutionally be reposed in a sovereign executive without endangering the limitations, checks, and balances upon which the constitutional system was grounded? Or, to put the question in another way: how much and what kinds of constitutional powers did the executive require to make possible the rational, purposeful, and powerful conduct of foreign affairs? A deep-felt suspicion of power in the American democratic tradition gave rise to another question: how could a democratic political order, reposing upon the "consent of the governed," be reconciled with intrinsic authoritarian necessities of foreign affairs?

The Problem of Inherent Power

An early constitutional question was whether, in fact, the authority and power to conduct foreign relations derived from the Constitution alone. Was the source of authority, as some suggested, possibly meta-constitutional? If so, then what possible restraints, other than political ones, could be imposed upon the exercise of powers derived from some law or authority beyond or above the Constitution itself?

The possibility was that both the power to conduct foreign relations and the supreme attribute of sovereignty itself arose because of the United States' sovereignty in the society of nations. This attribute and authority was inherited from its former possessor, the British Crown. Whether power had passed directly from the British Crown to the federal authorities of the new Republic or whether it came indirectly to those authorities via the individual states themselves (which, in the Constitution, supposedly had bequeathed them to the federal government), was somewhat beside the point. All states in the society of nations had such plenary powers. James Wilson first asserted the theory during the Constitutional Convention of 1787: "When the United States declared their independence, they were bound to receive the Law of Nations in its modern state of purity and refinement."[6]

This notion of inherent power, arising from the fact that the United States of America was a sovereign entity at international law, was elaborated by later American statesmen and jurists. In the hands of statesmen and Supreme Court Justices, the doctrine grew. America's entrance as a sovereign entity under international law implied the existence of a single government with unified and adequate power. Ironically it was Justice Sutherland, one of the willful "old men" of the Court of the 1930's (whose narrow conceptions of Presidential and federal power over domestic matters during the New Deal marked him as somewhat of a juridical troglodyte), who carried this meta-constitutional doctrine to its furthest extent. In the now-famous case of Curtiss-Wright in 1936 (a constitutional test of the extent of congressional and executive authority over foreign commerce), Justice Sutherland wrote:

A political society cannot endure without a supreme will somewhere. Sovereignty is never held in suspense. When, therefore, the external sovereignty of Great Britain in respect of the colonies ceased, it immediately passed to the union.[7]

---

[6] Quoted in Edwin S. Corwin, *The Presidency: Office and Powers*. New York: New York University Press, 1957, p. 172.

[7] 299 U.S. 304, 1936, pp. 316–17.

This possibility suggested extreme constitutional difficulties. It suggested that sovereign executive authority in foreign affairs, juridically speaking, drew strength from traditional laws of the universe of the society of nations. Yet in this universe of states at the time of the founding of the Republic, the conception of state sovereignty was all too tightly associated with Continental European conceptions of *Staatsraison* and *Machtpolitik*. In the eighteenth century society of nations, the dynastic states derived legitimacy from the "grace of God," not the "will of the people"; in practice these states assumed that state interests were fundamental and that their pursuit was the exclusive task of the sovereign statesman or ruler. The national or dynastic interest could thus be established by the ruler himself, his ministers, and his bureaucratic associates and translated into policy and action. Acts and declarations of war, treaties, alliances, peace itself, and the military and diplomatic maneuvering which all these involved were matters of *Grosse Politik*. Normally they were shrouded from public view by the majestic machinery of the state. They were subject to few constitutional restraints or limitations of the people and their elected representatives. The Continental European tradition thus stressed the unitary and authoritarian character of sovereign power in foreign relations. The people and their elected representatives, if any, had no legitimate role to play in the control and conduct of foreign policy. But then, they had no significant role to play in domestic policy either. The constitutional dilemma posed for the American Republic was, at the time, unique.

In the famous pseudonymic debate concerning Presidential foreign policy powers in 1793 between Hamilton and Madison, Madison (replying as *Helvidius* to Hamilton's *Pacificus*) accused Hamilton of seeking surreptitiously to invest the Presidency with the prerogatives of the British Crown:

> ... By whatever standard we try this doctrine, it must be condemned as no less vicious in theory than it would be dangerous in practice. It is countenanced neither by the writers on law; nor by the nature of the powers themselves; nor by any general arrangements ... to be found in the constitution.
>
> Whence then can the writer have borrowed it? There is but one answer to this question. The power of making treaties and

the power of declaring war, are royal prerogatives in the British government, and are accordingly treated as executive prerogatives by British commentators. . . .[8]

The particular issue then at stake concerned the constitutional justification of the President's power to proclaim neutrality in the war between France and England.

This constitutional novelty arose not just from the intrinsic tension between the Constitution as written document and the prevailing laws of the society of nations but from a qualitative difference between the American constitutional order and the traditional political orders of Europe out of which the laws of nations themselves had arisen. The American experiment, as its founders readily acknowledged, was unique. Democracy was to come into play. Such fundamental attributes of democracy as participation in law-making and popular consent to laws could not fail to flow over into the field of foreign affairs from the domestic realm wherein they were to play. Conversely, constitutional understandings pertaining to powers of the Presidency and the federal government in foreign relations could not help but profoundly influence and affect both democracy and republican practice.

No matter what the Hamiltonians, including Sutherland, wrote, there still were severe juridical limitations on federal and Presidential authority in foreign affairs which the Constitution made explicit. The society of nations to the contrary, Congress, not the President, had the constitutional power to declare a state of war. President and Senate were *jointly* empowered to use the treaty power for national purposes and objects, and in addition, the Constitution reserved certain powers and rights to the states and to the people. Could the President, perhaps, acting as the "federative power," or acting as Commander-in-Chief, or acting under the authority of the treaty-making power, then accomplish things which the Constitution otherwise forbade? The boundaries and frontiers of the individual states, for instance, could not be changed without the consent of the states concerned. Did this

---

[8] Quoted in Corwin, *op. cit.*, p. 180.

mean then that the Presidency and the "sovereign" federal authority by treaty could *not* do constitutionally what all other sovereigns, under the law of nations could: agree to international treaties and conventions affecting internal conditions within them? If a treaty, as the Constitution itself so stated, were to be regarded as the "supreme law of the land," could such law perhaps legitimately do things which ordinary Congressional law was constitutionally enjoined from doing? The Supreme Court case of *Missouri vs. Holland* in 1920 posed the issue: could a Congressional law implementing an Anglo-American conservation treaty vest in federal authorities regulatory powers within states for protection of game? Admittedly they had invaded a heretofore sacrosanct province of states' police powers which the Constitution until then protected. But the Court, through Holmes' decision, sustained the treaty, and revealed the possibility that:

> Acts of Congress are the supreme law of the land only when made in pursuance of the Constitution, while treaties are declared to be so when made under the authority of the United States. It is open to question whether the authority of the United States means more than the formal acts prescribed to make the convention. *We do not mean to imply that there are no qualifications to the tready-making power; but they must be ascertained in a different way* ... It is not lightly to be assumed that, in matters requiring national action, "a power which must belong to and somewhere reside in every civilized government" is not to be found ... The treaty in question does not contravene any prohibitory words to be found in the Constitution. The only question is whether it is forbidden by some invisible radiation from the general terms of the Tenth Amendment ... Here a national interest of very nearly the first magnitude is involved. It can be protected only by national action in concert with that of another power. . . .[9]

Justice Frankfurter once referred to some lawyers' habit in argumentation of displaying a "parade of the horribles." By this he meant that any power or law can be made to appear intolerable

---

[9] 252 U.S. 1920, p. 416. Quoted in *The Constitution of the United States of America, Analysis and Interpretation*, Washington, D.C.: U.S. Government Printing Office, 1953, pp. 428–429. (Italics mine.)

if one dwells long enough upon its intrinsic possibility of abuse. A parade of horribles could also be assembled from the motley possibilities of constitutional abuse, stalemate, and paralysis, which this whole matter of constitutional authority raised. Holmes might well have been right: when a national interest of the first magnitude was involved, the neat and tidy restraints of the Constitution seemed to give way to overriding necessity. But this did not eradicate the problem. It is always philosophically important to consider even constitutional problems *in extremis*.

As the Holmes decision points out, the exercise of the treaty power could conceivably be a constitutional battering-ram, possibly demolishing customary constitutional rights of states. But if, as *Missouri vs. Holland* seemed to suggest, the treaty power was a theoretical skeleton key to doors which even Congress was constitutionally forbidden to unlock, it could do even more. It might (as right-wing Brickerites loudly proclaimed in the 1950's) threaten even individual liberties of American citizens. Treaties might erode guaranteed rights of the due process of law, among others.

It was not only the treaty power itself (and the attendant power which the Presidency had long exercised in international relations, that of the executive agreement) which might do this. The executive agreement, a less pretentious but more prolific kind of international agreement than the treaty, is a creature of many forms, yet generally regarded as indispensable to the orderly conduct of foreign policy. One form of executive agreement is the international agreement between the U. S. government acting in executive capacity and some foreign state or international organization, binding upon the United States but not subjected to Senatorial consent. There are three particular subspecies: those which, as drafted, require and obtain Congressional legislative approval and implementation; those which are made, like many American commercial agreements, upon the basis of prior statutory authorization of Congress; and those which, like the Yalta agreement of 1945, are subject neither to prior Congressional "authorization," nor approval, nor subsequent consent. In practice as well as in theory, most really substantive international agreements entered into by the United States Government are both negotiated and designated by the Executive branch as treaties, but the Executive has wide, theoretical latitude in deciding what to call them. A cynic would define an executive agreement as any agreement not called a treaty by the President. But even exaggerating the iniquities of the White House, which might be tempted to dodge the difficulties of a Senatorial two-thirds by dressing an agreement in shabby clothing and slipping it in through the servants' entrance, there are good reasons why no Administration would, except in dire straits, play such tricks. For one thing, Senators are notoriously sensitive about prerogatives (including their treaty prerogative). For another, the act of Senatorial approval of international agreements endows the latter with more majesty than mere enactment by the President or mere approval by Congress as a whole, as with ordinary legislation. Thus Senatorial consent gives the substance of the act more authority by giving it greater repute in the international arena as well as in the minds of the American public. Brickerites and McCarthyites in the 1950's, who sought to curtail use of the executive agreement and the objects which treaties might properly deal with, ignored the administrative chaos which elimination of the executive agreement would bring about. They ignored, too, the real political restraints upon Presidential power in international agreements which required no constitutional amendment to come into being. They were amply there already.

The exercise of any one right or power by any branch of the federal government in foreign affairs could conceivably work mischief. Senator Henry Cabot Lodge and his colleagues proved this in 1919 when they killed Wilson's League and the Paris Peace Treaty. Willful, shrewd assassins in the Senate could use their treaty power like a stiletto, to dispose of a hated Chief Executive, even if the ensuing cost to the nation as a whole might be considerable. Conversely, any tyrant might envy the great powers of the President as Commander-in-Chief. . . . Their proper constitutional use depended in large measure on the character and purposes of those who possessed them. If there were possibilities of conflict and abuse of power among governmental institutions and such potential abuses were obvious, then conflict must be anticipated by responsible men, constantly aware of the dangers of national paralysis and disunity entailed in sustained partisan struggle.

But no Constitution could avert what Madison once called the "dangers of factionalism." Factionalism was inherent in political life. While its force and passion sometimes arose from petty interests and ambitions, factionalism might also be a reflection of deep substantive issues at stake in political choices. Political debates over institutional powers, the Constitution, and foreign policy, paralleled profound debates about national policy and purpose. Even honest political men could employ the Constitution to block some political purpose from its realization. What was unique in the American experience was that these passionate debates about constitutionalism and foreign affairs were arguments about what the existing Constitution was, what it said, or what it implied. The argument was not about *alternative* constitutional orders. The American Constitution was thus both the regulating mechanism of debate and conflict and a framework of dialogue which reasonable men welcomed.

Conflict over substantive foreign policy issues might thus appear as conflict or deadlock among constitutional entities. When this was so, substantive conflicts could masquerade as constitutional ones. When the will of one entity (the Presidency, for instance) threatened to carry the day on behalf of a particular policy or purpose, one way to inhibit the purpose was to challenge the constitutionality of that entity's behavior. Another was simply to exercise, to the fullest possible extent, the constitutional powers of other entities to block action. The frequency with which constitutional issues arose in periods of foreign policy crisis suggests that the debate over forms was one aspect of a debate over essentially non-constitutional matters (whether, as in 1793, to intervene against England in the Anglo-French war; whether, as in 1940, to intervene on behalf of England in the war between Hitler and the West). This suggested that the Constitution itself might at any time become the hapless prey of the institutions which it prescribed, or even worse, that the institutions themselves were prey of larger forces in the nation which the Constitution neither prescribed nor foresaw.

But before we turn to particular instances where this difficulty of interpretation was most dramatically revealed, we might point out a mitigating fact: the unity of the framework around which dispute took place — the Constitution itself. At no time in American history, not even during the Civil War, was the Constitutional framework itself attacked. In foreign affairs, particularly when great issues of the moment are at stake, the vigor of the constitutional debate over powers as such cannot be attributed to the substantive policy debate alone. Much more, it points to the desperate need in crisis to legitimize action and to link action and purpose to enduring forms and public values. The matter of constitutional legitimacy itself is no idle thing. Without it, power itself could easily dissolve in the hands of those who wield it. Worse still, the power might be wholly severed from constitutional authority and become despotic. Thus, in a sense, we can say that such recurrent constitutional debates were, in fact, *supremely* constitutional.

Questions

1. "The federative power necessary to the survival of a state has constantly endangered the organizational principles of a free society at all times." Discuss this statement in terms of the problem of dissent in the United States.

2. Is it true that democracy is not the best form of government to deal with foreign affairs? As a decision-maker, would you recommend subordinating domestic norms to international needs? As a politician running for Congress, could you, with impunity, advocate such subordination? Do you know any politicians that have done so? If so, what was their rationale?

3. Do you think the realities of world politics have made the separation of powers in the Constitution unworkable? Examine the Bricker Amendment. How would it relate to this question?

4. There are some interesting problems surrounding the issue of the powers of the several states versus the treaty-making power of the United States. Discuss them.

5. You are playing tennis; it is game, set, and match point. You meet the next volley from your opponent; but a sudden downdraft causes the ball to slam into the net and you lose the match. President Wilson may very well have felt similar frustrations after the Senate refused to accept the League of Nations. Must there be such obstacles to the treaty-making power? Is it useful to have internal structures, such as Senate approval of treaties, if most other nations have survived without such a structure? Is it practical? Should the President have unrestricted treaty power?

Chapter Two

The President and Foreign Policy

The foreign policy process in the United States is centered in the office, if not in the person, of the President. President Truman stated the case bluntly, albeit accurately: "I make foreign policy," he told a group of visitors. The simplicity of this truth obscures the complex nature of the American presidency, a fact often ignored by American, but readily apparent to foreign, observers. One of the most perceptive of the latter, Dennis Brogan, writing in *Encounter* soon after the assassination of President Kennedy, described the American president as a monarch — an elected monarch to be sure, but a monarch nonetheless. He was not, of course, thinking of the British crown as it exists today, shorn of all but its ceremonial powers, but of English monarchs in the sixteenth and seventeenth centuries who held, controlled, and exercised a full measure of political power.

This analogy between the roles of an American president and of a monarch who rules as well as reigns is persuasive precisely because the president is, just as British monarchs once were, simultaneously Head of State, Chief Executive, and leader of a political party. He thus combines, in his person, powers which English kings have long since lost and which many republics have been reluctant to entrust to their elected leaders. Seen through the lens of British constitutional development, it is little wonder that Brogan should find it meaningful to characterize the American president as a monarch with the implication of regal power and authority.

The roles of the President suggest the sources of his power over foreign affairs. The principal source is the Constitution which, in addition to bestowing all executive power on the President, makes him Head of State; thus, the President can lay effective claim to the right to speak for the nation. This claim is acknowledged, not only by most Americans, but also by other nations, and, except in unusual circumstances, the voice of the President is for them the voice of the United States. The President, therefore, controls the national "unity symbols" and can invoke the national honor and prestige in support of specific foreign policies in ways that no other policy-maker or political leader can.

In his constitutional office as Chief Executive, the President appoints administrators who not only help him make policy, but who also supervise the execution of policy. This control of the bureaucracy provides him with the machinery necessary to obtain and analyze the information essential to policy-making; it also permits him to withhold classified information from the legislature and the public. Because the President has access to secret information, Americans endow presidential opinions on foreign policy with credibility which can be overcome only through proof that he is suppressing or ignoring relevant information. This is usually difficult to do; Senator Keating persistently charged, in the summer and fall of 1962, that the Russians were planning to introduce offensive missiles into Cuba in the face of repeated administration denials, a reminder that presidential sources of information are not infallible.

In addition, the President obtains power over foreign affairs by virtue of his role as a political leader. Supplementing the force he possesses as a result of his formal positions, this political power increases his opportunities for bringing effective pressure to bear upon people he must rely on for support.

The President obtains maximum control over foreign policy only when he draws effectively on both sources of power — constitutional and political — and thus obtains an efficient "mix" of powers in terms of the problem at hand. The blending of these roles is, in itself, a source of presidential power; the President can limit criticism of those foreign policy decisions that are essentially politically motivated by donning the mantle of the Head of State. President Johnson's decision to participate in the Manila conference in early November 1966 was ascribed by his opponent to an attempt to influence the approaching elections, while his supporters were sure that it was an act of statesmanship designed only to further the cause of peace. The question of the real motive can be answered only by the President. But, as Head of State, his power over the formulation of foreign policy is enhanced by the tendency in American politics to follow the maxim, "Politics stop at the water's edge."

Each of these sources of presidential power over foreign policy implies, in turn, limitations on the President's power. Indeed, the limitations found in the Constitution on presidential control of foreign policy are more than implications. For the Constitution explicitly divides power in this area between the executive and the legislative branches. The division is not really balanced, to be sure, since the President is left with a substantial edge in power, but Congress is given some powers which can be ignored by the President only at the risk of having his policy rejected. Moreover, reckless use of the unity symbols by the President produces the "wolf, wolf" effect and causes the people to lose faith in the President. Hence, the President's effectiveness in manipulating public opinion and in handling political opposition by an appeal to national unity symbols rests, to a large extent, on its infrequent use.

The limitations on the President's other powers are not so formal but are nonetheless real. If control of the bureaucracy confers power on the President, it also constitutes a restriction on his power. For the bureaucracy is less like a tool to be used than like a living organism that must be nurtured and tended if it is to be useful. Therefore, the President must take the values of the bureaucracy into consideration in order to assure that his policies will be executed effectively and with zeal. The use of political power by the President to assure congressional and bureaucratic support for his foreign policy makes him vulnerable to political pressure from those he hopes to influence. President Eisenhower had to deal with a Democratic Congress for six of his eight years in office. In this situation, restraint in the use of political power was perhaps the only way he could obtain the necessary support for his policies. Wanton use of political power when in a position of strength exposes the President to retaliation when his position changes.

Finally, an additional limitation on the power of the President flows from the nature of the international system and the policies of his predecessors. American presidents since 1945 have been restricted in the alternatives available to them in foreign policy by the fact that World War II ended with only two great powers in the world. The existence of a "bipolar" world means that the United States will inevitably be the leader of the opposition to the other major power, unless, of course, it decides to opt out of international affairs. The cost of this leadership has been relatively heavy, and the United States has chosen to enter into a number of alliances in order to share the burden. These alliances have provided certain benefits, but at the same time they have restricted the United States' freedom to follow policies at odds with the interests of other members of the alliance. This restriction is as true for alliances with small states as

it is for those with larger, more powerful nations. It was clear in the For-
mosan straits crisis of 1958 that the United States would have preferred
to evacuate the off-shore islands of Quemoy and Matsu. This policy was
not followed because its ally, the Federal Republic of China, was determined to remain on the islands. The alternative then was to abandon the Nationalist Chinese to the mercy of the Chinese Communists or to continue
such support as was necessary to assure that they retained control of the
islands. In view of this alliance structure, only the latter policy was viable.
Certainly it was possible for the President to elect to do otherwise, but the
realities of the international system sharply reduced the chances of his
doing so. After all, the "objective" world has to be dealt with in its own
terms, not in terms of the President's choosing. Harry Truman did not
create Stalin; Franklin Roosevelt did not will Hitler into existence; John
Kennedy was not consulted by the Russians before they placed their missiles in Cuba; and Lyndon Johnson does not dictate the foreign policy of
the USSR. The international system forms the external environment of
presidential decisions on foreign policy and forces the President to forsake
the search for the ideal and to settle for what is possible in an imperfect
world.

Since the role of the President is crucial in the foreign policy process,
the readings were chosen to probe and to illuminate the central problems of
that role; this section should be studied with some care. In the first reading, "The President," Professor Louis W. Koenig offers a succinct review
of the President's constitutional and legal powers. A clear understanding
of these is, of course, the solid foundation of fact on which any further
analysis must be based.

Richard E. Neustadt, in "Sources of Presidential Power," contrasts
the clerkship and the leadership possibilities inherent in the constitutional
and political powers of the President. He makes the telling point that reliance solely on the formal powers necessarily limits the leadership potential of the office. Rather, the combination of these powers with the
"power to persuade" confers the mantle of leadership upon the President.
Note also Neustadt's fivefold classification of the clients whom the President must satisfy in the pursuit of his duties.

The Neustadt discussion is a general statement of the problems of the
President in fulfilling the role of the "leader." James McGregor Burns, in
"Foreign Policy Leadership," focuses sharply on the role of the President
in foreign affairs. He highlights the problem of presidential decision-making
with appropriate examples and thus forces the reader to come to grips
with the essential elements of foreign policy making at the presidential
level.

The President*

Louis W. Koenig

Louis W. Koenig, Professor of Political Science at New York University, has been consultant to the Department of State and the first Hoover Commission. He has also been associate of and consultant to the Ford Foundation. He is the author of *Invisible Presidency, Presidency Today, Official Makers of Public Policy,* and *Public Administration.*

Director of Foreign Policy

The Constitution goes far toward making the President a chief diplomat. Several Presidents have candidly expressed satisfaction with their foreign-affairs powers. Thomas Jefferson termed the conduct of foreign affairs "executive altogether," and Harry Truman once flatly asserted, "I make foreign policy." Although Congress, mindful of its powers in a constitutional system of separation of powers and checks and balances, would disagree, both Presidents boasted of significant accomplishments in foreign affairs in their respective administrations — Jefferson the Louisiana Purchase and the Embargo, and Truman the "Truman Doctrine," the European Recovery Program, the North Atlantic Treaty, and the Point Four Program.

In actuality, many of the President's foreign-affairs powers are shared with Congress, particularly the Senate. The President makes treaties, with the advice and consent of the Senate, "provided two-thirds of the Senators present concur." The Senate can reject a treaty outright or impose conditions or reservations which may or may not be acceptable to the President. When the test-ban treaty was under Senate review, President Kennedy dispatched a letter to the chamber carrying "unqualified and unequivocal assurances" that the treaty would not deter him from maintaining a

*Reprinted from *Official Makers of Public Policy: Congress and the President* by Louis W. Koenig. Copyright © 1965 by Scott, Foresman and Company.

vigorous weapons program. Kennedy gave other assurances, including one that the treaty would never be altered by executive action but only by treaty procedure. The President's pledge headed off threatened Senate reservations. The President may shun the treaty procedure and resort to executive agreements, which entail no Senate review. The President can make executive agreements with other nations by exercising his independent authority or "prerogative," such as his power as commander in chief and as possessor, under the Constitution, of the executive power. Statutes and treaties also may authorize executive agreements. President Roosevelt's exchange of United States destroyers for British bases in World War II was an executive agreement based upon the commander-in-chief power, the executive-power clause, and a statute authorizing the transfer of "obsolescent" military material.

The President, according to the Constitution, nominates, and, with the Senate's advice and consent, appoints ambassadors and ministers. The Constitution empowers the President to receive the diplomatic representatives of other nations; this power enables him to recognize new governments. By implication, he can demand the recall of foreign diplomats, as Washington did Citizen Genêt, the representative of revolutionary France. Although the Constitution empowers Congress to declare war, presidential war-making is a longstanding adjunct of foreign policy, embracing Jefferson's dispatching of naval frigates to tame the Tripolitan pirates to Kennedy's 1962 imposition of a naval blockade around Cuba. But presidential war-making, as the Korean conflict demonstrates, can be hazardous politically. In time, the American people tired of the Korean venture; in the 1952 elections they rejected the continuation of a Democratic presidential administration. The victor, Dwight D. Eisenhower, when faced in his subsequent administration with crises in Formosa and the Middle East that might assume the proportions of the Korean conflict, moved to couple Congress in his policy determinations concerning those troubled areas and thereby hoped to share with the legislative branch any subsequent political liabilities that might materialize. The resolutions that Congress passed authorized the President to use the armed forces "as he deems necessary for the specific purpose of securing and protecting Formosa and the Pescadores against armed attack." Congress passed a comparable resolution for the Middle East.

For the President, playing an effective role in foreign policy depends not a little upon his ability to induce foreign leaders — whether friend, foe, or neutral — to accept his policies. The President is the formulator and negotiator of major foreign-policy objectives: to keep other nations out of the Communist orbit, to build a structure of nuclear interdependence among our allies, and to persist in negotiations with the Communist world as a preferable alternative to armed conflict. President Kennedy's foreign visitors in his first year could be counted by the score. He also corresponded with a wide circle of foreign leaders on major problems. The summit conference, at which the President confers with allied or Communist leaders, or both, has become a standard presidential experience: Roosevelt at Yalta, Truman at Potsdam, Eisenhower at Geneva, Kennedy at Vienna.

Since World War II, the President has had to superintend a series of alliances encircling the globe, from NATO in the west to SEATO in the east. The President is often the chief sponsor and promoter of major shifts in alliance policy. Truman pushed West Germany's rearmament and inclusion in the NATO system. Kennedy and Johnson championed a NATO missile fleet manned by crews of various nationalities.

The President's policy concerns with affairs of an ally may reach the point where he moves to effect change in its government. President Kennedy in 1963 was faced with a badly deteriorating war in South Vietnam and the threat which that situation posed to his own domestic political welfare in the United States. To halt the trend of events in South Vietnam, Kennedy sought to encourage the removal of Ngo Dinh Nhu, whose influence over his brother-in-law, President Ngo Dinh Diem, appeared related to South Vietnam's faltering military performance. In a public statement, Kennedy attributed South Vietnam's failings to its government's loss of touch with the people and suggested the desirability of "changes in policy and perhaps with personnel." President Diem's regime was subsequently overthrown, he and his brother-in-law were murdered, and the "changes" of "personnel" proceeded.

Commander in Chief

The President's constitutional power and responsibility as commander in chief thrust him into a variety of major policy-making capacities. He may be the principal architect of military campaigns. Lincoln, for example, selected points of attack in the Civil War, and Franklin Roosevelt conceived the North African invasion and chose its landing points in World War II. The nuclear age has securely established the President as the nation's principal field commander. He alone under law decides when to use nuclear weapons. The dread possibility of nuclear conflict has thrust upon him the making of many decisions that in a simpler military age fell upon local commanders. Thus Kennedy in the 1962 Cuban crisis, after the imposition of a blockade, was kept apprised of the whereabouts of approaching Communist vessels and personally gave the order to board them.

As commander in chief, the President can also terminate hostilities by arranging an armistice and entering into agreements with the nation's allies to set the framework of the postwar order. Woodrow Wilson thus incorporated his Fourteen Points into the armistice for World War I. Franklin Roosevelt arranged through his personal efforts and those of his field commanders the demarcation of occupation zones, including those for Berlin — which in actuality established areas of continuing hegemony for the Communist and allied powers after World War II.

As commander in chief, the President appoints and removes field commanders. Such acts may be fraught with policy consequences. President Truman dramatically removed General Douglas MacArthur from his command in the Korean War. In a series of public statements, MacArthur had attacked the established administration policy of restricted war and urged instead broadened military action against Red China, including a blockade, air bombardment, and ultimately, invasion. The General also advocated the use of Chinese Nationalist forces, which the administration was determined to avoid. At stake in these policy differences were the authority of the President and civil supremacy over the military in policy-making. "In view of the specific responsibilities imposed upon me by the Constitution of the United States and the added responsibility to the United Nations," Truman said in announcing MacArthur's removal, "I have decided that I must make a change of command in the Far East. . . . It is fundamental . . . that military commanders must be governed by the policies and directives issued to them in the manner provided by our laws and the Constitution." [1]

As commander in chief, the President may make policy of the utmost consequence for domestic society — for individual freedom, for the functioning of our governmental processes, and for property rights. The most drastic of these assertions occurred in the Civil War, particularly in the war's first weeks, when Congress was not in session. Lincoln, acting as commander in chief, and solely on his own authority, added twenty-three thousand men to the Regular Army and eighteen thousand to the Navy; called forty thousand volunteers for three years' service; summoned the state militias into a ninety-day volunteer force; paid $2 million from the Treasury's unappropriated funds for purposes unauthorized by Congress; closed the Post Office to "treasonable correspondence"; imposed a blockade on southern ports; suspended the writ of habeas corpus in certain parts of the country; and caused the arrest and military detention of persons engaging in or contemplating "treasonable practices."

In World War II, under the commander in chief's authority, some 112,000 persons of Japanese ancestry — of whom 70,000 were United States citizens — were removed from the West Coast to "relocation centers" in the interior. The commander in chief also may seize property. Six months before Pearl Harbor, President Roosevelt, while the nation was still officially at peace, seized the strike-bound North American Aviation plant at Inglewood, California. Roosevelt based his seizure upon the "duty constitutionally and inherently resting upon the President to exert his civil and military as well as his moral authority to keep the defensive efforts of the United States a going concern" and "to obtain supplies for which Congress has appropriated money, and which it has directed the President to obtain." Other seizures, both before and during our belligerent status, followed. In the Korean conflict, however, President Truman's seizure of most of the nation's steel mills was declared unconstitutional by the Supreme Court.

---

[1] Harry S. Truman *Memoirs*, Garden City, New York, Doubleday & Company, Inc., 1955-56, II, p. 449.

Labor, too, has felt the force of the commander in chief power. President Roosevelt in World War II created a War Manpower Commission, with responsibilities for both the Selective Service System and the manpower needs of war-production industries. The WMC quickly adopted a "work or fight" policy, which forced all workers engaged in "non-essential enterprise to choose between induction into the armed forces and transfer to war-production jobs.

Questions

1. The power of the President to initiate military activities without a formal declaration of war by the Congress is a long-established practice. What constitutional justifications are there for it? Are there any limitations on this power, i.e., financial control by the Congress? Have these powers of limitation been generally used? Why or why not?
2. It has been suggested that the United States have two presidents: one for foreign affairs and one for domestic. Comment on this proposal.

Sources of Presidential Power*

Richard E. Neustadt

Richard E. Neustadt was named special consultant to President Kennedy in 1961. Before this, he had been consultant to the United States Senate Subcommittee on National Policy Machinery and special assistant to the White House (1950 - 1953) under President Truman. He is Associate Dean of the Graduate School of Public Administration and Director of the Institute of Politics, both of Harvard University. He has taught at Columbia and Oxford universities.

In the United States we like to "rate" a President. We measure him as "weak" or "strong" and call what we are measuring his "leadership." We do not wait until a man is dead; we rate him

---

*Reprinted with permission, from *Presidential Power* by Richard E. Neustadt, 1960, John Wiley & Sons, Inc.

from the moment he takes office. We are quite right to do so. His office has become the focal point of politics and policy in our political system. Our commentators and our politicians make a specialty of taking the man's measurements. The rest of us join in when we feel "government" impinging on our private lives. In the third quarter of the twentieth century millions of us have that feeling often.

. . . Although we all make judgments about presidential leadership, we often base our judgments upon images of office that are far removed from the reality. We also use those images when we tell one another whom to choose as President. But it is risky to appraise a man in office or to choose a man for office on false premises about the nature of his job. When the job is the Presidency of the United States the risk becomes excessive. . . .

We deal here with the President himself and with his influence on governmental action. In institutional terms the Presidency now includes 2,000 men and women. The President is only one of them. But *his* performance scarcely can be measured without focusing on *him*. In terms of party, or of country, or the West, so-called, his leadership involves far more than governmental action. But the sharpening of spirit and of values and of purposes is not done in a vacuum. Although governmental action may not be the whole of leadership, all else is nurtured by it and gains meaning from it. Yet if we treat the Presidency as the President, we cannot measure him as though he were the government. Not action as an outcome but his impact on the outcome is the measure of the man. His strength or weakness, then, turns on his personal capacity to influence the conduct of the men who make up government. His influence becomes the mark of leadership. To rate a President according to these rules, one looks into the man's own capabilities as seeker and as wielder of effective influence upon the other men involved in governing the country. . . .

. . . .

There are two ways to study "presidential power." One way is to focus on the tactics, so to speak, of influencing certain men in given situations: how to get a bill through Congress, how to settle strikes, how to quiet Cabinet feuds, or how to stop a Suez. The other way is to step back from tactics on those "givens" and to deal with influence in more strategic terms: what is its nature and what are its sources? What can *this* man accomplish to improve the prospect that he will have influence when he wants it? Strategically, the question is not how he masters Congress in a peculiar instance, but what he does to boost his chance for mastery in any instance, looking toward tomorrow from today. The second of these two ways has been chosen for this book.

To look into the strategy of presidential influence one must decide at whom to look. Power problems vary with the scope and scale of government, the state of politics, the progress of technology, the pace of world relationships. Power in the Nineteen-sixties cannot be acquired or employed on the same terms as those befitting Calvin Coolidge, or Theodore Roosevelt, or Grover Cleveland, or James K. Polk. But there is a real likelihood that in the next decade a President will have to reach for influence and use it under much the same conditions we have known since the Second World War. If so, the men whose problems shed most light on White House prospects are Dwight David Eisenhower and Harry S. Truman. . . . To do so is to see the shadow of another, Franklin D. Roosevelt. They worked amidst the remnants of his voter coalition, and they filled an office that his practice had enlarged.

.   .   .   .

In form all Presidents are leaders, nowadays. In fact this guarantees no more than that they will be clerks. Everybody now expects the man inside the White House to do something about everything. Laws and customs now reflect acceptance of him as the Great Initiator, an acceptance quite as widespread at the Capitol as at his end of Pennsylvania Avenue. But such acceptance does not signify that all the rest of government is at his feet. It merely signifies that other men have found it practically impossible to do *their* jobs without assurance of initiatives from him. Service for themselves, not power for the President, has brought them to accept his leadership in form. They find his actions useful in their business. The transformation of his routine obligations testifies to their dependence on an active White House. A President, these days, is an invaluable clerk. His services are in demand all over Washington. His influence, however, is a very different matter. Laws and customs tell us little about leadership in fact.

Why have our Presidents been honored with this clerkship? The answer is that no one else's services suffice. Our Constitution, our traditions, and our politics provide no better source for the initiatives a President can take. Executive officials need decisions, and political protection, and a referee for fights. Where are these to come from but the White House? Congressmen need an agenda from outside, something with high status to respond to or react against. What provides it better than the program of the President? Party politicians need a record to defend in the next national campaign. How can it be made except by "their" Administration? Private persons with a public axe to grind may need a helping hand or they may need a grinding stone. In either case who gives more satisfaction than a President? And outside the United States, in every country where our policies and postures influence home politics, there will be people needing just the "right" thing said and done or just the "wrong" thing stopped in *Washington.* What symbolizes Washington more nearly than the White House?

A modern President is bound to face demands for aid and service from five more or less distinguishable sources: from Executive officialdom, from Congress, from his partisans, from citizens at large, and from abroad. The Presidency's clerkship is expressive of these pressures. In effect they are constituency pressures and each President has five sets of constituents. The five are not distinguished by their membership; membership is obviously an overlapping matter. And taken one by one they do not match the man's electorate; one of them, indeed, is outside his electorate. They are distinguished, rather, by their different claims upon him. Initiatives are what they want, for five distinctive reasons. Since government and politics have offered no alternative, our laws and customs turn those wants into his obligations.

Why, then, is the President not guaranteed an influence commensurate with services performed? Constituent relations are relations of dependence. Everyone with any share in governing this country will belong to one (or two, or three) of his "constituencies." Since everyone depends on him why is he not assured of everyone's support? The answer is that no one else sits where he sits, or sees quite as he sees; no one else feels the full weight of his obligations. Those obligations are a tribute to his unique place in our political system. But just because it is unique they fall on him alone. *The same conditions that promote his leadership in form preclude a guarantee of leadership in fact.* No man or group at either end of Pennsylvania Avenue shares his peculiar status in our government and politics. That is why his services are in demand. By the same token, though, the obligations of all other men are different from his own. His Cabinet officers have departmental duties and constituents. His legislative leaders head *congressional* parties, one in either House. His national party organization stands apart from his official family. His political allies in the States need not face Washington, or one another. The private groups that seek him out are not compelled to govern. And friends abroad are not compelled to run in our elections. Lacking his position and prerogatives, these men cannot regard his obligations as their own. They have their jobs to do; none is the same as his. As they perceive their duty they may find it right to follow him, in fact, or they may not. Whether they will feel obliged *on their responsibility* to do what he wants done remains an open question. . . .

In the early summer of 1952, before the heat of the campaign, President Truman used to contemplate the problems of the General-become-President should Eisenhower win the forth-coming election. "He'll sit here," Truman would remark (tapping his desk for emphasis), "and he'll say, 'Do this! Do that!' *And nothing will happen.* Poor Ike — it won't be a bit like the Army. He'll find it very frustrating."

Eisenhower evidently found it so. "In the face of the continuing dissidence and disunity, the President sometimes simply exploded with exasperation," wrote Robert Donovan in comment on the early months of Eisenhower's first term. "What was the use, he demanded to know, of his trying to lead the Republican Party. . . ." And this reaction was not limited to early months alone, or to his party only. "The President still feels," an Eisenhower aide remarked to me in 1958, "that when he's decided something, that *ought* to be the end of it . . . and when it bounces back undone or done wrong, he tends to react with shocked surprise."

Truman knew whereof he spoke. With "resignation" in the place of "shocked surprise" the aide's description would have fitted

Truman. The former senator may have been less shocked than the former general, but he was no less subjected to that painful and repetitive experience: "Do this, do that, and nothing will happen." Long before he came to talk of Eisenhower he had put his own experience in other words: "I sit here all day trying to persuade people to do the things they ought to have sense enough to do without my persuading them. . . . That's all the powers of the President amount to."

In these words of a President, spoken on the job, one finds the essence of the problem now before us: "powers" are no guarantee of power; clerkship is no guarantee of leadership. The limits on command suggest the structure of our government. The constitutional convention of 1787 is supposed to have created a government of "separated powers." It did nothing of the sort. Rather, it created a government of separated institutions *sharing* powers. "I am part of the legislative process," Eisenhower often said in 1959 as a reminder of his veto. Congress, the dispenser of authority and funds, is no less part of the administrative process. Federalism adds another set of separated institutions. The Bill of Rights adds others. Many public purposes can only be achieved by voluntary acts of private institutions; the press, for one, in Douglass Cater's phrase, is a "fourth branch of government." And with the coming of alliances abroad, the separate institutions of a London, or a Bonn, share in the making of American public policy.

What the Constitution separates our political parties do not combine. The parties are themselves composed of separated organizations sharing public authority. The authority consists of nominating powers. Our national parties are confederations of state and local party institutions, with a headquarters that represents the White House, more or less, if the party has a President in office. These confederacies manage presidential nominations. All other public offices depend upon electorates confined within the states. All other nominations are controlled within the states. The President and congressmen who bear one party's label are divided by dependence upon different sets of voters. The differences are sharpest at the stage of nomination. The White House has too small a share in nominating congressmen, and Congress has too little weight in nominating Presidents for party to erase their constitutional separation. Party links are stronger than are frequently supposed, but nominating processes assure the separation.

The separateness of institutions and the sharing of authority prescribe the terms on which a President persuades. When one man shares authority with another, but does not gain or lose his job upon the other's whim, his willingness to act upon the urging of the other turns on whether he conceives the action right for him. The essence of a President's persuasive task is to convince such men that what the White House wants of them is what they ought to do for their sake and on their authority.

Persuasive power, thus defined, amounts to more than charm or reasoned argument. These have their uses for a President, but these are not the whole of his resources. For the men he would induce to do what he wants done on their own responsibility will need or fear some acts by him on his responsibility. If they share his authority, he has some share in theirs. Presidential "powers" may be inconclusive when a President commands, but always remain relevant as he persuades. The status and authority inherent in his office reinforce his logic and his charm.

Status adds something to persuasiveness; authority adds still more. . . . In Walter Bagehot's charming phrase, "no man can *argue* on his knees." Although there is no kneeling in this country, few men — and exceedingly few Cabinet officers — are immune to the impulse to say "yes" to the President of the United States. It grows harder to say "no" when they are seated in his oval office at the White House, or in his study on the second floor, where almost tangibly he partakes of the aura of his physical surroundings. . . .

A President's authority and status give him great advantages in dealing with the men he would persuade. Each "power" is a vantage point for him in the degree that other men have use for his authority. From the veto to appointments, from publicity to budgeting, and so down a long list, the White House now controls the most encompassing array of vantage points in the American political system. With hardly an exception, the men who share in governing this country are aware that at some time, in some degree, the doing of *their* jobs, the furthering of *their* ambitions, may depend upon the President of the United States. Their need for presidential action, or their fear of it, is bound to be recurrent if not actually continuous. Their need or fear is his advantage.

A President's advantages are greater than mere listing of his "powers" might suggest. The men with whom he deals must deal with him until the last day of his term. Because they have continuing relationships with him, his future, while it lasts, supports his present influence. Even though there is no need or fear of him today, what he could do tomorrow may supply today's advantage. Continuing relationships may convert any "power," any aspect of his status, into vantage points in almost any case. When he induces other men to do what he wants done, a President can trade on their dependence now *and* later.

The President's advantages are checked by the advantages of others. Continuing relationships will pull in both directions. These are relationships of mutual dependence. A President depends upon the men he would persuade; he has to reckon with his need or fear of them. They too will possess status, or authority, or both, else they would be of little use to him. Their vantage points confront his own; their power tempers his.

. . . .

The power to persuade is the power to bargain. Status and authority yield bargaining advantages. But in a government of "separated institutions sharing powers," they yield them to all sides. With the array of vantage points at his disposal, a President may be far more persuasive than his logic or his charm could make him. But outcomes are not guaranteed by his advantages. There remain the counter pressures those whom he would influence can bring to bear on him from vantage points at their disposal. Command has limited utility; persuasion becomes give-and-take. It is well that the White House holds the vantage points it does. In such a business any President may need them all — and more.

This view of power as akin to bargaining is one we commonly accept in the sphere of congressional relations. Every textbook states and every legislative session demonstrates that save in times like the extraordinary Hundred Days of 1933 — times virtually ruled out by definition at mid-century — a President will often be unable to obtain congressional action on his terms or even to halt action he opposes. The reverse is equally accepted: Congress often is frustrated by the President. Their formal powers are so intertwined that neither will accomplish very much, for very long, without the acquiescence of the other. By the same token, though, what one demands the other can resist. The stage is set for that great game, much like collective bargaining, in which each seeks to profit from the other's needs and fears. It is a game played catch-as-catch-can, case by case. And everybody knows the game, observers and participants alike.

. . . .

Influence becomes still more a matter of give-and-take when Presidents attempt to deal with allied governments. A classic illustration is the long unhappy wrangle over Suez policy in 1956. In dealing with the British and the French before their military intervention, Eisenhower had his share of bargaining advantages but no effective power of command. His allies had their share of counter pressures, and they finally tried the most extreme of all: action despite him. His pressure then was instrumental in reversing them. But had the British government been on safe ground *at home*, Eisenhower's wishes might have made as little difference after intervention as before. Behind the decorum of diplomacy — which was not very decorous in the Suez affair — relationships among allies are not unlike relationships among state delegations at a national convention. Power is persuasion and persuasion becomes bargaining. The concept is familiar to everyone who watches foreign policy.

In only one sphere is the concept unfamiliar: the sphere of executive relations. Perhaps because of civics textbooks and teaching in our schools, Americans instinctively resist the view that power in this sphere resembles power in all others. Even Washington reporters, White House aides, and congressmen are not immune to the illusion that administrative agencies comprise a single structure, "the" Executive Branch, where presidential word is law, or ought to be. Yet we have seen . . . that when a President seeks something from executive officials his persuasiveness is subject to the same sorts of limitations as in the case of congressmen, or governors, or national committeemen, or private citizens, or foreign governments. There are no generic differences, no differences in kind and only sometimes in degree. . . .

Like our governmental structure as a whole, the executive establishment consists of separated institutions sharing powers. The President heads one of these; Cabinet officers, agency administrators, and military commanders head others. Below the departmental level, virtually independent bureau chiefs head many more. Under mid-century conditions, Federal operations spill across dividing lines on organization charts; almost every policy entangles many agencies; almost every program calls for interagency collaboration. Everything somehow involves the President. But operating agencies owe their existence least of all to one another — and only in some part to him. Each has a separate statutory base; each has its statutes to administer; each deals with a different set of subcommittees at the Capitol. Each has its own peculiar set of clients, friends, and enemies outside the formal government. Each has a different set of specialized careerists inside its own bailiwick. Our Constitution gives the President the "take-care" clause and the appointive power. Our statutes give him central budgeting and a degree of personnel control. All agency administrators are responsible to him. But they *also* are responsible to Congress, to their clients, to their staffs, and to themselves. In short, they have five masters. Only after all of those do they owe any loyalty to each other.

"The members of the Cabinet," Charles G. Dawes used to remark, "are a President's natural enemies." Dawes had been Harding's Budget Director, Coolidge's Vice-President, and Hoover's Ambassador to London; he also had been General Pershing's chief assistant for supply in the First World War. The words are highly colored, but Dawes knew whereof he spoke. The men who have to serve so many masters cannot help but be somewhat the "enemy" of any one of them. By the same token, any master wanting service is in some degree the "enemy" of such a servant. A President is likely to want loyal support but not to relish trouble on his doorstep. Yet the more his Cabinet members cleave to him, the more they may need help from him in fending off the wrath of rival masters. Help, though, is synonymous with trouble. Many a Cabinet officer, with loyalty ill-rewarded by his lights and help withheld, has come to view the White House as innately hostile to department heads. Dawes's dictum can be turned around.

A senior presidential aide remarked to me in Eisenhower's time: "If some of these Cabinet members would just take time out to stop and ask themselves 'What would I want if I were President?', they wouldn't give him all the trouble he's been having." But even if they asked themselves the question, such officials often could not act upon the answer. Their personal attachment to the President is all too often overwhelmed by duty to their other masters.

. . . .

Granting that persuasion has no guarantee attached, how can a President reduce the risks of failing to persuade? How can he maximize his prospects for effectiveness by minimizing chances that his power will elude him? The Marshall Plan suggests an answer: he guards his power prospects in the course of making choices. Marshall himself, and Forrestal, and Harriman, and others of the sort held office on the President's appointment. Vandenberg had vast symbolic value partly because F.D.R. and Truman had done everything they could, since 1944, to build him up. The Treasury Department and the Budget Bureau — which together might have jeopardized the plans these others made — were headed by officials whose prestige depended wholly on their jobs. What Truman needed for those "givers" he received, in part, because of his past choice of men and measures. What they received in turn were actions taken or withheld by him, himself. The things they needed from him mostly involved his own conduct where his current choices ruled. The President's own actions in the past had cleared the way for current bargaining. His actions in the present were his trading stock. Behind each action lay a personal choice, and these together comprised *his* control over the give-and-take that gained him what he wanted. In the degree that Truman, personally, affected the advantages he drew from his relationships with other men in government, *his power was protected by his choices.*

By "choice" I mean no more than what is commonly referred to as "decision": a President's own act of doing or not doing. Decision is so often indecisive and indecision is so frequently conclusive, that choice becomes the preferable term. "Choice" has its share of undesired connotations. In common usage it implies a black-and-white alternative. Presidential choices are rarely of that character. It also may imply that the alternatives are set before the choice-maker by someone else. A President is often left to figure out his options for himself. Neither implication holds in any of the references to "choice" throughout this book.

If Presidents could count upon past choices to enhance their current influence, as Truman's choice of men had done for him, persuasion would pose fewer difficulties than it does. But Presidents can count on no such thing. Depending on the circumstances, prior choices can be as embarrassing as they were helpful in the instance of the Marshall Plan. The incidents described [earlier] . . . include some sharp examples of embarrassment. Among others: Eisenhower's influence with Faubus was diminished by his earlier statements to the press and by his unconditional agreement to converse in friendly style at Newport. Truman's hold upon MacArthur was weakened by his deference toward him in the past.

Assuming that past choices have protected influence, not harmed it, present choices still may be inadequate. If Presidents could count on their own conduct to provide them *enough* bargaining advantages, as Truman's conduct did where Vandenberg and Marshall were concerned, effective bargaining might be much easier to manage than it often is. In the steel crisis, for instance, Truman's own persuasiveness with companies and union, both, was burdened by the conduct of an independent Wage Board and of government attorneys in the courts, to say nothing of Wilson, Arnall, Sawyer, and the like. Yet in practice, if not theory, many of *their* crucial choices never were the President's to make. Decisions that are legally in others' hands, or delegated past recall, have an unhappy way of proving just the trading stock most needed when the White House wants to trade. One reason why Truman was consistently more influential in the instance of the Marshall Plan than in the steel case, or the MacArthur case, is that the Marshall Plan directly involved Congress. In congressional relations there are some things that no one but the President can do. His chance to choose is higher when a message must be sent, or a nomination submitted, or a bill signed into law, than when the sphere of action is confined to the Executive, where all decisive tasks may have been delegated past recall.

But adequate or not, a President's own choices are the only means *in his own hands* of guarding his own prospects for effective influence. He can draw power from continuing relationships in the degree that he can capitalize upon the needs of others for the Presidency's status and authority. He helps himself to do so, though, by nothing save ability to recognize the pre-conditions and the chance advantages and to proceed accordingly in the course of the choice-making that comes his way. To ask how he can guard prospective influence is thus to raise a further question: what helps him guard his power stakes in his own acts of choice?

Questions

1. Richard E. Neustadt says that presidential power is the power to persuade. Comment and give instances when this has occurred.
2. The President creates his own role as leader but he cannot avoid being clerk at the same time. What factors determine his role as clerk and is it possible for him to reject this role? If so, at what cost?
3. Many people on both sides of the political fence have charged that President Eisenhower was less effective than he could have been because he was too nonpolitical. Whether this is true or not, it is obvious that many people expect partisanship from the President. Can a President remain aloof from partisan politics in his foreign policy decisions? Should he?

Foreign Policy Leadership*

James McGregor Burns

James McGregor Burns, Professor of Government at Williams College, has written a number of important books including *Congress on Trial, Roosevelt: the Lion and the Fox, John Kennedy: a Political Profile, Presidential Government,* and *The Deadlock of Democracy: Four-Party Politics in America.*

The Framers of the Constitution planned that the President would have broader powers in shaping and executing foreign

---

*Reprinted, with permission, from *Presidential Government*, by James McGregor Burns, 1965, Houghton Mifflin Company.

policy than domestic. Recognizing the special need for speedy and single-minded executive action, they made it possible for the President to be the main spokesman for the nation and the master of the two key agencies of foreign policy, the diplomatic corps and the armed forces. They granted him in effect complete discretion to recognize or not recognize foreign governments. Constitutional usage has sanctioned even stronger presidential power. While the President under the Constitution shares his treaty-making power with the Senate, he can on his sole discretion make executive agreements with foreign nations, and these agreements, unless overturned by Congress, have virtually the same legal validity as treaties in the eyes of the courts. Even at a time when the Supreme Court was circumscribing the President's authority in domestic affairs it was upholding sweeping presidential authority over foreign relations. In 1936 the court recognized the "very delicate, plenary and exclusive power of the President as the sole organ of the federal government in the field of international relations — a power which does not require as a basis for its exercise an act of Congress, but which, of course, like every other governmental power, must be exercised in subordination to the applicable provisions of the Constitution." [1] The President can make, entirely on his own, statements that may rock every chancellery on earth. He can quietly set in motion various approaches and feelers and trial balloons that could have a profound impact on international relationships. He has the power to react to world events in such a way as to prolong and intensify cold war or to plunge the nation and the world into a nuclear hot war. The power of Congress to make a declaration of war has become hardly more than a formality.

Despite all this, Professor Warren concluded after a study of the President's world leadership in this century, "ironically, in a period when the presidency is at the very peak of its influence, probably nowhere in the world is executive leadership more hemmed in, more limited by political considerations, more vulnerable to pressures from within and without than in the United States. For one, Congress by no means has been relegated to a minor position in foreign policy. Farflung commitments involve

---

[1] *United States* v. *Curtiss-Wright Export Corporation*, 299 U.S. 304.

the Senate in treaty-making functions, and both Houses in appropriating funds for the vast operational programs overseas.... Limitations on presidential power come also from the opposing party, from his own party, from the press, and from various organs of public opinion. All of these make his job the most difficult and complicated balancing act on earth while he tries to lead the nation through global agitations that, beyond his capacity to subdue, he can only try to prevent from erupting disastrously." [2]

The seeming paradox of the President's sweeping formal powers over foreign policy and the actual restrictions on him can be resolved in part if we distinguish once again between his powers of management and his capacity for innovation and leadership. Much of the President's daily activity is simply a balancing act. The President's latitude is very narrow. As Sorensen has suggested, he must make choices within narrow limits of permissibility, available resources, time, previous commitments, and available information.[3] On the other hand, over the years a kind of policy machine has evolved to handle — to "manage" — foreign problems and even crises.

A disturbance abroad brings into play a vast and interlocked system of interaction and adjustment. Intelligence streams into the White House security room, the State Department, the Pentagon, the Central Intelligence Agncy. Quick consultations take place over the telephone; staffs assemble; conferences are set up. Queries and instructions are flashed to men in the field, to our embassies abroad, to foreign embassies in Washington. Our missions at the United Nations and other international agencies, such as NATO, are alerted and consulted. Within the larger departments background material is worked up, precedents examined, specialists called in, various proposals and solutions canvassed. In an acute crisis, the President can communicate directly with heads of foreign powers.

The Cuban missile crisis in 1962 demonstrated how well the system can work under the most intense pressure. Decisions were

---

[2] Sidney Warren, *The President as World Leader* (Philadelphia: J. B. Lippincott Company, 1964), pp. 431–32.

[3] Theodore Sorensen, *Decision-Making in the White House* (New York: Columbia University Press, 1963), p. 23.

made not by a "lonely President" somewhere off in an eyrie but were hammered out day after day by fourteen or fifteen men meeting in the White House or the State Department, with the Chief Executive not even present most of the time. The group perfectly exemplified the decision-making processes of the modern Presidency; it was composed of old Eisenhower and Stevenson men and new Kennedy men, of presidential Democrats and Republicans, of White House staff members and representatives from CIA and the State and Defense Departments. The group operated in part through committees and subcommittees. It analyzed Khrushchev's possible strategies, a variety of possible responses from Washington, how Moscow would react to those responses, and how the American people and their government might react to those reactions. Options were kept open on each side so that neither would be forced into a corner. Communications were widened to friends, foes, and neutrals. A presidential speech was drafted, circulated, redrafted. The President talked by telephone with former Presidents Hoover, Truman, and Eisenhower. Congressional leaders were informed, though hardly consulted. The group finally had to recommend a choice between limited and unlimited action. Acting by consensus, it recommended the former, and the President agreed.

. . . .

Whatever exact pattern consultation will follow, it has one vital effect. A wide variety of persons with different views and perspectives become involved. To consult is to ask advice, and to ask advice is to imply at least some need for consent. Even a Washington official's act of merely informing another office in Washington or a ministry abroad provides a kind of access to decision making that the other party may exploit. Thus this system of communication and adjustment incorporates its own checks and balances. At the very least the system produces delays during which tempers may cool and further communication and adjustment may take place.

This system of clearing and adjusting and conciliating is indispensable for a world of sovereign nations. But it is one that binds the President rather severely. At best he can act only as a master broker, trying to find some common denominator among a host of differing ideological camps, national interests, party attitudes, issue-oriented groups, bureaucratic claims, and policy specialists. Often the President may not have any policy goal of his own; his aim is a compromise, a settlement, a reduction of tensions. He may be as impersonal about the substance of the final compromise, within certain limits, as he is about the settlement of a labor conflict that has been projected into the White House by a threatened nationwide walkout in a critical industry. Adjustment is an object in itself.

Of a very different order is a President's initiative in the face of a far more generalized, remote, and novel situation. Guidelines are lacking; the flow of intelligence is uncertain or even contradictory; presidential estimates must turn on future contingencies and present imponderables. Yet some kind of action, some kind of decision, seems imperative either because of the likely urgency of the future situation or because the President must take action at the time, when options might be open, rather than wait until choices have been greatly narrowed.

. . . .

Truman's decision to use the atomic bomb against Japan is [an] ... example of taking an epochal step in the face of many imponderables. Truman, Secretary of State James F. Byrnes, and Secretary of War Henry Stimson had to calculate the immediate military advantages of using atomic warfare against Japan. Among these were the extent of the shock effect on a nation already jolted by severe air attacks; whether the shock effect would harden Japan's will to resist or weaken it; the likely military and civilian casualties resulting from atomic attack as compared to those that would occur after an invasion using conventional weapons; and above all, the saving of American lives as a result of atomic attack. Then there were the possible secondary effects of dropping the bomb: the immediate reaction of national and world opinion; the prospects of defeating Japan before the Russians became heavily involved; the effect on our other wartime allies; the dire need that would arise after the war of restraining the use of atomic power — putting the genii back into the bottle — and the difficulties of achieving this once one nation had used the bomb for immediate military purposes. And then there were the long-term implications of dropping the bomb: the creation of a precedent that could be used some time by another nation; the atomic arms race that might ensue; the spiral of international suspicion that might blight postwar hopes. Scientists who had worked on the bomb, and who by their own mode of thought were deeply concerned with the remote long-term effects of dropping it, had warned that the military advantages of the bomb and the saving of American lives might be outweighed by the resulting loss of world confidence in the United States and by a "wave of horror and repulsion" sweeping over the rest of the world.

Truman made his decision almost exclusively on the basis of the more immediate, military, and calculable criteria. Dropping the two bombs did help bring about an early Japanese offer to lay down arms; the losses in the two bombings, awful though they were, probably were less than an orthodox invasion would have caused; and Japan gave up at a time when the Americans could exploit their military power in Japan proper in dealing with the Russians. But there were also the longer-term consequences. A feeling of revulsion swept the world; Russian and Chinese communists exploited the unilateral American act for propagandistic purposes; an atomic, and later a nuclear, arms race got under way; and it proved difficult if not impossible to put the genii back into the bottle. Such was a passing verdict twenty years after the event; the verdict one hundred years later might be quite different.

The issue here is not the rightness of Truman's act (or of his later decision to begin the manufacture of nuclear weapons). The question that concerns us is the manner in which Truman made his judgment. As a typically pragmatic American politician he dealt with the tangible features of the situation, the immediately probable results. Inevitably his bias was toward the more short-run and controllable elements of the equation. No matter how compelling the longer-term implications of dropping the bomb might have seemed, they posed such huge imponderables and contingencies that they defied easy calculation. The bias was toward immediate results, short-run implications, calculable sequences of action.

Today we can assess some of the longer-run effects of the

decision. Surprise use of the bomb did create a precedent that was available indefinitely to any bellicose member of the growing family of nuclear nations. An atomic and nuclear race did ensue (as it probably would have anyway). Not only the Communists but unilateralist and pacifist groups in friendly and neutral nations had a fine propaganda weapon against the United States. And the fear and hysteria aroused by the bomb's effects and sustained by the development of advanced delivery systems hardened peoples' attitudes and immensely complicated international efforts to control the production and deployment of nuclear weapons.

Yet the earlier presidential decision and the resulting tendencies were not irreversible. In 1963 Kennedy conducted his remarkable effort to achieve a limited test ban treaty with the Russians and other powers. Prospects had seemed especially bleak in the wake of the erection of the Berlin wall and of the stiff encounter — and Soviet withdrawal — in the Cuban missile crisis. Kennedy used all the resources of the Presidency in sounding out the Russians, pressing the negotiations, informing and guiding American public opinion, and pushing the treaty through the Senate. The treaty was only a small step, as Kennedy emphasized. But it was part of what he saw as a long-run and purposeful effort at relaxation of dangers and tensions as a prelude to more comprehensive international efforts to improve economic and political relations among nations.

Roosevelt's Lend-Lease program, Truman's decision on the bomb, Truman's military and foreign aid programs, Kennedy's breakthrough on control of nuclear weapons — these and countless other examples of presidential leadership remind us of the inevitable long-run implications of action and inaction. The most prudent and practical short-run step may widen the alternatives of a later President or drastically narrow them. Dwight Eisenhower's refusal to take any significant step in the face of the long-recognized world population explosion may be seen some day as one of the most crucial acts — or non-acts — of his administration. Long-run calculations may produce catastrophes as a result of overcommitment or poor planning; they may also alter the political context so significantly that future Presidents gain an immensely broadened discretion.

These considerations may throw light on the paradox noted

earlier . . . — the fact that presidential power in foreign affairs seems so limited even while it is obviously so wide. Each view is correct; everything depends on what the President is trying to do and by what measures his actions are evaluated. In his efforts at day-to-day adjustments he is severely limited by the ineluctable circumstance that he must operate in a world of sovereign nations and through rather old and cumbersome machinery for foreign policy making and action. In this regard, however, he may enjoy considerable latitude, under the Constitution and under custom, from Congress, the opposition party, and the press. In his long-range planning he may find ways of overcoming international restraints if his proposals — like Point Four — are daring, idealistic, and generous. But in such planning he may run into political obstacles at home, especially from congressional and other conservative forces concerned about excessive political and financial commitments abroad. Often his proposals are both short-run and long-run and hence meet a variety of responses in Congress and in foreign capitols.

All things considered, the President has a vast potential for leadership abroad. The huge bureaucratic and other institutional forces that surround and sometimes frustrate him are also powerful instruments for implementing his decisions. The world of divided peoples is also a world yearning for inspired leadership. The events that seem so intractable, like the emplacement of missiles in Cuba or a raging inflation in Latin America, can also be made to open up grand opportunities. Much depends on the energy, tenacity, and resourcefulness of the central decision makers and presidential politicians — on presidential government. And much depends on the availability and accessibility of new ideas and of the men who produce them.

Questions

1. "The President . . . must make choices within narrow limits of permissibility." Does this mean that political factors will always necessarily limit even the most determined President?

2. Do you think improved communications technology has been beneficial to the foreign policy process, or has it just served to obscure the issues by flooding the executive branch with data?

3. You are listening to a nomination speech at a national party convention. The nominator says: "Our leader, Calvin Delano Washington, is a man who has a clear record of no-compromise in foreign policy. If elected, he will change things." Is this a realistic approach to foreign policy?

Chapter Three

Congress and Foreign Policy

The framers of the Constitution clearly acted on the assumption that the conduct of foreign policy is, by its nature, an executive function. Nevertheless, they limited executive control by granting to Congress several specific powers over foreign policy; among these was the power, granted to the Senate, to give its advice and consent to the appointment of "ambassadors, consuls and other public ministers" and to the ratification of treaties. Congress, as a whole, was given the power to raise and maintain armies and navies and to declare war. Despite these congressional privileges, the division of power over foreign affairs in the Constitution is heavily weighted in favor of the executive. Moreover, the powers granted to Congress do not add up to a clearly defined role. Congress is therefore without guidelines as to how and when its right to restrict executive discretion should be used. What role can and should Congress play? This question is at the heart of the relationship of Congress to foreign policy.

In the past, Congress has vacillated between two sharply different roles. The first requires close congressional supervision over all levels of foreign policy. In this view, not only is congressional participation in fixing broad national goals considered desirable, but congressional involvement in the details of policy is seen as necessary if Congress is to avoid the label "rubber stamp." This involvement is thought to require congressional review and approval of policy decisions, not only on the entire range of substantive issues, but also on the details of recruitment, selection, and assignment of personnel in foreign affairs agencies and, in particular, careful review of the budgets of these agencies. Consequently, programs requiring large expenditures of funds are subjected to scrutiny to determine their relevance to broader foreign policy goals, their feasibility, and how their funds could most efficiently be used. Moreover, it is argued that Congressional supervision must continue beyond the policy formulation stage to the execution stage.

The second role which Congress has seen for itself in foreign affairs has recognized as necessary and legitimate legislative participation in the fixing of broad national goals but has thought congressional involvement in the details of policy unnecessary. In this view, Congress shares with the executive the responsibility for establishing what Walt Rostow has called the "national style." This concept involves, in addition to national goals, the determination of the spirit in which those goals are pursued. If this task is performed well, the details of achieving goals can safely be left to the executive, with Congress conducting periodic reviews to assure that national goals are meaningful and that the executive decisions remain relevant to those goals and reflect the "national style" as fixed by legislative-executive cooperation.

If Congress is to opt for the first role, it must undertake a reorganization and a re-examination of its own structure and processes which would aid the emergence of a congressional consensus. This task would be difficult enough if it were only a question of executive-legislative relations, but inextricably intertwined with this relationship is the interparty conflict which often casts the President as the leader of a political struggle whose arena is Congress. Therefore, congressional unity must surmount this additional, and perhaps insurmountable, obstacle.

Two further conditions would seem to be necessary if Congress is to supervise and review in detail the formulation and execution of foreign policy: (1) Congress would need resources to conduct meaningful studies of foreign policy proposals. This would probably mean a considerable reorganization of the existing committee system to concentrate power over foreign affairs in a minimum of committees. The staff of these committees would have to be increased substantially in size, since the complexity of the issues involved in foreign affairs requires careful consideration by staff members with an expertise at least equal to that of the officials in the executive branch. (2) Congress would have to solve the information problem. At present Congress is faced with the dilemma of having simultaneously both too much and too little information. The problem of too much information is essentially the problem of small staffs. The amount of information which must be sifted and analyzed is too large a burden for the existing staffs. Enlarging the staffs and upgrading their quality would contribute substantially to the ability of Congress to reduce the information relevant to foreign policy decisions to manageable proportion.

This would not, however, solve the problem of too little information. Much of foreign policy is made on the basis of classified information. If Congress were to exercise a really meaningful supervision of the details of policy it would have to have access to this information. But American presidents have been reluctant to share this information with Congress and have on occasion evoked their right to withhold information from Congress when they considered that its release would not be in the national interest. To the extent that the executive has "better" information than Congress, its power over foreign affairs must remain paramount if for no other reason than that "Knowledge is power." Therefore, unless Congress could solve the information problem, its efforts to supervise closely the details of policy appear to be unrealistic.

The nature of the legislative process and the present structure of Congress suggests that the second role is the more realistic. First, perhaps, because little real unity exists in Congress. Who speaks for Congress? Instead of one voice there are several, each of which reflects some portion of Congress and each of which denies that the others are authentic expressions of congressional will. This multitude of voices cannot hope to compete with the executive branch, which, while not perfectly unified, presents a relatively solid front to Congress and the nation. The divisions within Congress give the executive ample opportunity to rely on the tried and true rule, "Divide and conquer."

The second, and perhaps, the most important reason, is that the restrictions on the ability of Congress to deal with the details of foreign policy do not apply when Congress turns its attention to the broad outlines of policy. Robert Dahl has suggested why this is so:

> . . . the more closely debate moves toward broad and basic policy, the more competent is the legislative decision likely to be, and correspondingly less competent is the expert. This is not merely because basic policy involves "value" questions which ought to be outside the political authority of the expert in a democracy. It is also because the judgments of "fact" must include more and more complex variable on which the expert, in the present state of social sciences, is probably professionally less competent than the intelligent politician. When questions of military strategy

broaden into problems of international politics, as they inevitably will at some point, the competence of the general ought to give way to that of the politician . . .[1]

If the foregoing is accurate, our national style in the formulation of foreign policy should include intense executive-legislative cooperation in fixing broad foreign policy goals. This cooperation will assure that those goals reflect a national consensus which will serve as a frame of reference for policy-makers and for the development of bipartisan foreign policy. Most important, it appears to offer a solution to the emergence of a "constitutional dictatorship" in foreign policy. As Dahl has pointed out, such a dictatorship is perhaps inevitable unless "Congress can be converted into a basic institution for deciding what and whose preferences are to guide the conduct of foreign affairs."

If this goal is to be achieved, the reform must begin with the committee system since it is here that the "real" work of Congress is done. The key, therefore, to the understanding of Congress and foreign policy is to understand the way that committees operate and their relationship to the Senate and the House as a whole. Consequently, the first two articles in this section concentrate on the politics and behavior of these committees. "The Congress and National Security Policy" by Holbert N. Carroll describes the changes in the environment and organization of Congressional action during the past thirty years. Carroll is careful to note the splintering of supervision over foreign policy in Congres and that this division is reflected in the multiplicity of committees dealing with foreign policy. The second piece, Carroll's "The Politics of the Committees," discusses the impact of the committee system on the decision-making process.

In the final selection, Senator J. W. Fulbright asks the same question as did Professor Dahl: What should be Congress' role in foreign policy? He expresses his concern that, over the past twenty years, presidential control of foreign policy has increased at the expense of Congress, particularly at the expense of the Senate. The speech concludes with some suggestions for halting the erosion of congressional influence and re-establishing the constitutional balance between congressional and executive control of foreign policy.

---

[1] From Robert A. Dahl, *Congress and Foreign Policy* (New York: Harcourt, Brace & World, Inc., 1950), pp. 244–45.

The Congress and National Security Policy*

Holbert N. Carroll

Holbert Nicholson Carroll was educated at the University of Pittsburgh and at Harvard. He was a consultant to the Brookings Institution, Washington, D. C., and is presently Chairman of the Department of Political Science at the University of Pittsburgh.

To one President, the demand of the House of Representatives for executive correspondence relating to negotiations with another nation, and the threat of the House to refuse funds to implement the commitment, jeopardized the balances of the Constitution. In a major address, he later solemnly warned the nation about the hazards of dissension, partisanship, and prejudice in foreign policy.

To another President, a House action would be the signal for other nations "whether they are to deal with a strong or a weak President." He admonished the representatives that the amendment to deny him discretion "places handcuffs upon the President and leaves the key in the possession of a body of men who cannot possibly act with the speed frequently required in international negotiations." [1]

Both Presidents prevailed. President Washington in 1796 overcame a defiant House on the Senate-approved Jay Treaty. In 1963, President Johnson got the discretion he sought to underwrite Soviet credit for the purchase of American wheat.

These events, separated by 167 years, reveal the persistent tension of the political system between the requirements of a Constitution dividing and limiting the powers of government and addressed primarily to the achievement of "domestic tran-

---

*In *The Congress and America's Future*, David B. Truman, Ed., © 1965 by The American Assembly, Columbia University, New York, N. Y. Reprinted by permission of Prentice-Hall, Inc., Englewood Cliffs, New Jersey.
[1] *New York Times*, December 24, 1963.

quillity" and the exigencies of conducting the external affairs of the nation. Today, the formal allotment of powers between the President and the Congress remains exactly as when the Constitution was adopted. The allotment compels, and tradition supports, congressional participation in defining both the domestic and external purposes of the nation and in achieving the goal of national security, always fervently shared by the President and the Congress. Presidential dominance in conducting the external relations of the nation and congressional preoccupation with the domestic tasks of perfecting the Union represented a rough accommodation through history to the tension of the system. National security was the happy sum of their efforts. It was a general goal like freedom or justice. It rarely demanded concentrated attention.

Radical changes in the requirements of national security, especially since the 1930s, have spurred fresh adjustments to the tension of the political system of divided and shared power, now so inextricably drawn into the fantastically complex affairs of every part of the globe. From the President's perspective, national security policy spans that range of national policies identified in a summary way in the tasks of the National Security Council to advise him on the integration of "domestic, foreign, and military policies relating to the national security...."[2] His perspective is thus the whole of national policy as it bears on relations with foreign nations.

For the Congress the boundaries are more confined. To the Congress national security policy is preeminently military policy and much of foreign policy. In these sectors the Congress generally acquiesces in presidential dominance. Its mode of behavior, by necessity or choice, has become primarily that of monitoring the executive branch. Looking back from the third decade of the revolution in the requirements of national security, the increasing tendency to monitor, to establish political perimeters of tolerance and expectation, rather than to use power to intervene deeply in shaping the substance of policies, is perhaps the most striking development in congressional behavior.

Between the presidential and congressional perceptions of

---

[2] 61 Stat. 496, Section 101(a).

national security policy lies an ill-defined area. The President strikes a national security theme, but the Congress often does not. Even then, the Congress more often than not asserts its voice on the periphery of fundamentals. These are policies which the Congress views as marginal to national security, as essentially domestic and thus essentially congressional. Or the policies involve cherished powers, such as the power of the purse, for purposes that the Congress is reluctant to accept as continuing necessities of national security. Setting sugar import quotas, tariff issues, restricting immigration, disposing of farm surpluses abroad, internal security problems, cultural and informational programs, and, in significant ways, foreign aid are examples of policy areas in which the Congress is more assertive. Needless to add, the Congress gives continuing detailed attention to the administrative organizations through which policies are implemented.

Regardless of the depth of its involvement, whether it chooses to monitor, to attempt to govern, or, more commonly, to blend the two tendencies in varying proportions, the Congress participates significantly in the shaping of national security policies. No major legislature in the world can match the extent of its participation.

The Environment

Fractions of Power

The number and variety of programs needed to support the multiple dimensions of national security involve a large number of the committees and other groupings in the fragmented power structure of the Congress. In justifying continuing foreign-military programs in a typical year of the 1960s, the Secretaries of State and Defense were obliged to maintain close relationships with ten major committees. Important programs or issues also were likely to rest in the jurisdictions of some fifteen other committees.

These standing and joint committees spawned more than seventy subcommittees. A few of the subunits required continuing attention by the Secretaries and their subordinates. Each year, for example, the House Appropriations Subcommittee on Foreign Operations took hundreds of hours of testimony in reviewing foreign aid programs. Thousands of man hours were consumed in preparing for these annual reviews.

In addition to their relationships with many committees and subcommittees, the Secretaries necessarily maintained critical ties with key individuals, with chairmen, with ranking minority committeemen, and with the majority and minority party leaders.

The number and diversity of congressional units invariably acts as a restraint on policy. Fragmentation inspires caution and complicates the search for consensus. So many bases have to be touched and so many points exist where programs and policies can be eroded that an administrator is more likely to choose the conservative approach than one innovating and departing from past patterns. The annual foreign aid programs are reviewed and revised by five units of the Congress and intermittently concern as many as thirty other committees and subcommittees. At least nine fractions of the Congress are interested in the administration of the Department of State. A missile problem can easily spur activity by eight major committees.

Duplication of effort is common. Several committees can intervene, or fail to act, and complicate the conduct of policy. In 1960, for instance, President Eisenhower sought flexibility in using sugar quotas as leverage in conducting relations with Castro's Cuba and the Dominican Republic, then under Trujillo. The President had the general support of congressional foreign policy leaders. He worked closely with other Latin American states.

The President got discretion with regard to Cuba, but the Congress, approving bills reported by the farm committees, required increased purchases of Dominican sugar. When the Dominican government was condemned by the Organization of American States for acts of aggression against Venezuela, the President requested authority to cut back the Dominican allotment. The farm committees could not agree on a bill. Inaction required the President to allot the substantial sugar bonus to the Dominican Republic.

Innovations in Organization

Organizational responses to the new demands of national security have largely been carried out within the traditional committee structure, as modified by the reorganization of 1946. Improved staffing and the proliferation of specialized subcommittees have been the principal organizational changes.

The historic centers of major influence have retained their dominant positions. These include the House and Senate Armed Services Committees (formed in 1947 from the Military and Naval Affairs committees), the Appropriations Committees, and the Senate Committee on Foreign Relations. The Appropriations Committees, and especially subcommittees of the House money group, have gained more influence because of the requirement of substantial funds to support foreign-defense programs. With the new importance of the House, the Committee on Foreign Affairs, with a rich tradition but little business until the 1930s, has gained stature.

Three committees have emerged to cover major new sectors of policy that could not be readily accommodated within the traditional structure. The House Committee on Science and Astronautics and the Senate Committee on Aeronautical and Space Sciences, organized in 1959, are concerned with the largely non-military aspects of outer space, as reflected in the programs of the National Aeronautics and Space Administration. Space issues are not easily compartmentalized into the military and the non-military. It is not surprising that military policy issues pervade the deliberations of the space units as well as the other committees — Armed Services, Appropriations, and Atomic Energy — more directly specializing in such matters.

The third new major unit, the Joint Committee on Atomic Energy, organized in 1946, has developed into perhaps the most powerful and influential standing committee that the Congress has ever created. It is unique. Joint House-Senate committees are rare. They normally have been given only study and reporting functions. The Joint Committee on Atomic Energy, in contrast, reports legislation to either the House or the Senate. Its recommendations are rarely challenged. Its power and influence in the atomic energy sector, which extends significantly into the realms of international diplomacy, are only in a minor way reflected in the business it presents to the House and the Senate. It is of greater importance that the committee has woven itself into the processes of executive deliberation, thus breaking down the nor-

mal barriers between the executive and legislative aspects of decision-making.

Modifications of Behavior

The Congress processes foreign-military business in much the
same way as other public business, but distinctive modes of behavior are displayed in dealing with the basic programs and
policies which the Congress embraces as requirements of national
security. Recognition of the special roles and burdens of the
President, the element of secrecy, the bewildering technology, the
hazards in choosing wrongly, the penchant to avoid responsibility,
the involvement of foreign nations and cultures, the necessities
of multilateral diplomacy, appeals to national unity and interest
transcending local and partisan considerations — these and other
factors inspire more caution and restraint by the Congress, its
parts, and the members than is evident in the handling of other
public business.

The restraints are reflected in the behavior of the majority
of the members. Senators and representatives enjoy greater freedom from constituent and other pressures in exercising judgment
about responses to the foreign environment than they do in such
matters as farm and welfare programs and civil rights. The congressman who chooses to exploit his greater freedom in disrup-
tive, irresponsible way gets extraordinary publicity. The more
prevalent pattern of individual behavior, one more important
ultimately in the congressional impact upon policy, is disciplined
restraint.

Caution and restraint also are evident in the extensive bipartisanship pervading the consideration of foreign-military
policy business. While comprehensive bipartisanship, in the sense
of close Republican-Democratic collaboration beginning in the
early stages of policy initiation, is rare, the less dramatic forms
of bipartisanship in a committee, in floor debates, in votes on
critical issues, and in the often private contacts with the President and his subordinates have been routine in the processing
of national security business.

Other factors in the new dimensions of national security condition the behavior of the Congress and uniquely color its de-

liberation. Because his powers and, especially, his responsibilities in acting for the nation in the world are directly affected by what the Congress does or fails to do, the President more deeply and frequently involves himself in this aspect of the legislative process than he ordinarily does. Congressional deliberations also are affected by the increasing intervention of foreign nations and their publicity agents in the political processes of the national government, by the revolution in transportation and in communications that permits committees and members to be in Viet-Nam or the Congo during crises or to talk with Soviet leaders within a few hours of flying from Washington, and by the occasional assignment of Senators and representatives to diplomatic roles at international meetings.

.   .   .   .

The Future

.   .   .   .

The Concerns of the Congress

Much important activity in the military and foreign policy realms lies beyond any really effective control or influence by the Congress and its parts. The Congress often is relatively passive, moreover, concerning foreign-military developments and situations that it could influence.

Congressional concern, and thus the extent of its activities, is closely related to the extent of public concern. If an issue or situation interests only small publics, only a few members are likely to carry on a dialogue with them. As the attentive publics grow in size and variety, and especially as mass media join to dramatize issues and problems, more members, committees, and subcommittees become active. When concern spreads down from the attentive elements to affect the general public, the temperature of the Congress rises rapidly.

This correlation of congressional and public concern may be illustrated with regard to Viet-Nam. During the 1950s elements in the Congress only intermittently monitored the commitment of the United States. General legislative support was implied by annual approval of the foreign aid programs. In 1954 the negative reaction of Republican and Democratic congressional party leaders was perhaps decisive when they were consulted by the administration concerning proposals to use American planes and warships to help the French on the eve of the Dien Bien Phu defeat. In 1959 a series of newspaper articles charging aid mismanagement spurred House and Senate subcommittee investigations in Washington and in Saigon. A few members of the Congress visited Viet-Nam in the 1950s, but only one, Senator Mike Mansfield, gave continuing attention to the situation. In the eyes of the administration, his voice at times was the voice of the Congress. Only with the extensive commitment of men and resources beginning in 1961 did concern and activity spread from a few to many members of the Congress.

In allotting time, energy, and thought, the great majority of the members of the Congress give higher priority to domestic problems and programs than to the nation's international involvements. Each member it, of course, intensely concerned about the nation's physical security. The big votes for defense appropriations underscore this concern. The members also are quite involved in such domestic national security business as defense contracts. They worry about foreign policy.

Except for the specialists on the committees processing the principal legislative ingredients of national security policy, however, the members focus on the more familiar and politically more important domestic issues. For the member and his constituents, programs to achieve international goals are often unpleasant competitors for resources that might support domestic programs. The human tendency is to give the unpleasant lower priority. The flood of programs demanding the congressman's attention, coupled with the fact that most are mired in a huge volume of constituent business that they choose to perform, virtually guarantees a low priority for international business.

Reform

This scale of priorities is only one of several problems troubling those most sensitive to the world responsibilities of the United States and most concerned about the future of the Congress. While conceding that, in many respects, the Congress has adapted remarkably well and that its adaptability provides a basis for optimism about the future, it can be argued that the Congress displays major deficiencies that weaken the effectiveness of national security policies and programs and impair legislative influence and control in their formulation and execution.

The deficiencies most commonly noted stem from the dispersal of power and the lack of ways for coordinating judgments on interrelated programs and policies. Military, industrial, political, scientific, cultural, diplomatic, economic, psychological, and other factors are now woven together in the formulation and implementation of foreign-military policies. While the Congress has attempted to cope with these realities — the *ad hoc* joint hearings by the Senate's Armed Services and Foreign Relations Committees on the Test Ban Treaty and the Cuba and Formosa resolutions are examples — more commonly it responds or fails to respond to parts of interrelated problems as the diffuse structure and the specialized interests and impulses of committees, subcommittees, and individual members dictate.

Problems that once could be regarded as wholly domestic in their implications but that now bear critically on the nation's international obligations, moreover, are managed by committees which, while increasingly alert to the international aspects of their business, concede excessively to domestic pressures. Use of the executive budget for coordinated discussion and action is, of course, prevented by the congressional practice of splitting the budget into numerous parts for review and action.

The dispersal of related business among a multitude of isolated compartments and inadequate thought to the interdependence of programs and policies not only affect the substance of policies and their implementation; these practices also drain an inordinate amount of the time and energy of public officials.

In looking to the future, it is evident that foreign-military programs and policies will become infinitely more complex and require extraordinary degrees of sophistication and coordination by the executive and legislative branches in their formulation and execution. Scientific and technological considerations — even now often beyond the layman's grasp — will become increasingly dominant. The political system will be confronted by unparalleled tests. If the Congress fails to adapt adequately and imaginatively to this state of affairs, a further decline in its influence is in prospect. Ill-equipped to participate in making critical judgments, it may abdicate fundamental aspects of its representative functions. Its efforts to keep the executive accountable may become a hollow formality. On occasion, it may strike out irrationally to affect programs and policies in ways that might be dangerous for the nation.

These and other diagnoses of the ills of the Congress have provoked a variety of proposals for reform. For some, the extent of the illness requires drastic surgery, nothing less than amendment of the Constitution to provide for a fusion of executive and legislative power as in Great Britain. Disciplined majorities, the direct and continuing confrontation of coordinated executive programs and legislative power, the executive weapon of dissolution — these and other features of the ideal parliamentary system, so it is argued, offer the only adequate cure for the deficiencies of the system of separated, fragmented, checked, and balanced powers in a totally unprecedented era of world affairs.

Less drastic alternatives for the Congress lie in various proposals for a better utilization of the resources of the political parties. The members of the Congress generally resist the prospects of greater party discipline. While the recipes differ, virtually every analysis of the Congress concludes that party reform offers the most promising opportunities for the Congress to arrest its decline, to enhance its voice in public affairs, and to mitigate the hazards of uncoordinated, fragmented, undisciplined, and, at times, irresponsible exercises of power.

Political parties are the only agencies of the Congress that have general, continuing responsibility for everything that the Congress does or fails to do. On many occasions in the past, party leadership has demonstrated the capacity for enhancing the stature of the Congress on the world scene. Yet, the potential of party resources for the development of consensus, for coordinating policies and programs throughout the legislative process, with the executive branch, and between the parties, and generally for promoting greater discipline and responsibility to offset the disintegrated structure of the Congress has only barely and intermittently been exploited.

Proposals for party reform are linked with others that promise a more unified and constructive role for the Congress. The proposals include expansion of professional staff resources, experiments with a periodic question period in each chamber or before joint meetings of both houses, frequent use of joint committees and joint subcommittees within and between the houses in related policy areas, and formation of a joint committee on national security.

An answer to the question of whether the Congress is adequately staffed depends upon one's conception of its roles and functions. Those opposed to a major staff expansion fear that the search for consensus would be complicated. The Congress could never hope to match executive expertise, but its attempts might result in the development of rival foreign-military policies and dramatically weaken the Executive's tasks in managing relations with the world.

Proponents argue that a failure to expand staff resources will lead to a further decline in the competence and influence of the Congress. As scientific and technological factors increasingly intrude into the shaping and implementation of foreign-defense programs, laymen, whether part of the attentive public, administrators in the executive branch, or congressmen, become increasingly less competent to evaluate them. Unless the Congress is adequately staffed, its options are to take the word of executive expertise — to which the political leaders of the executive branch have perhaps already succumbed in bewilderment — or to stab out haphazardly, irrationally, and in frustration. In either event, the loss is a loss for democratic government.

From this perspective, the Congress should dramatically expand its staff resources. One proposal, for example, urges formation of an institute or academy of experts to advise the Congress and its parts. The academy would draw upon university and other sources of knowledge. The congressional experts would have a vested interest in disagreeing with and testing the recommendations of the executive branch. They could look ahead, plan, and anticipate situations. In the competition and testing, laymen in and out of the Congress would derive a sounder basis for exercising that fundamental, humanizing quality which can be summed up in one word — *wisdom.*

Discussion of reform prospects by members of the Congress has most commonly centered on the proposal for an integrating committee on national security policy. Many variations of the idea have been advanced. Most attention has been given to the formation of a Joint Committee on National Security Policy, composed of members drawn from the House and Senate committees — Armed Services, Appropriations, Foreign Relations, Foreign Affairs, Atomic Energy, Space — with jurisdiction over the principal elements of national security policy. The joint group's domain would parallel that of the National Security Council.

As most commonly advocated, the joint group would not supplant the standing committees. It would study, inquire, review, investigate, and report, giving primary attention to the inter-relationships among policies and programs that relate to national security. The group's activities, so the proponents of the reform argue, would fill an information void for the Congress and especially provide coordinated perspectives to guide the members and many standing committees and subcommittees at work on aspects of national security policy. The group could also serve as a high-level vehicle for communication between the executive and legislative branches. Only rarely do the proponents explore whether the joint group might possibly develop into a powerful competitor of the President.

In Conclusion

Looking back from the third decade of the revolution in the requirements of national security, it is evident that major changes have occurred in aspects of congressional behavior. The demands of international politics have inevitably enhanced executive power. Drawing upon resources that the Congress could not expect to match, the President initiates and coordinates the major programs and policies that relate to national security. He calculates where the nation's interests lie. The Congress provides legitimacy for these calculations. Regarding fundamental aspects of national security policy, the dominant inclinations of the Congress have become to test, to criticize, to publicize, to compel explanations and justifications, in a word, to monitor. While by no means a certainty in a system of divided and diffused power, the evidence indicates that these trends in congressional behavior will gradually embrace a broader range of policies and programs that bear on the nation's international involvements. Whether in the process the Congress will gain or lose stature, power, and influence will be determined in large measure by the Congress itself.

In reality, national security policy is a blend of all of the nation's policies as they affect the world roles of the United States. It is inseparable from other sectors of public policy. Whether the United States enjoys domestic tranquillity, the blessings of liberty, security, and the other purposes for which the Constitution was ordained depends upon how successfully and imaginatively the political system, including the Congress, responds to the fantastic pace and scope of change in the United States and in the world. Politics and public policy have inextricably become both national and international.

Questions

1. Should Congress "intervene deeply in shaping the substance of policies," or do you think its monitoring function should be the extent of its activities in foreign policy?
2. It has been charged that federal administrators often choose a conservative approach to many issues, for fear that an innovative one might offend "the powers that be." Who are "the powers that be"? If the President gets pretty much what he wants from the Congress on foreign policy issues, why should foreign policy administrators worry about congressional power centers?
3. Professor Carroll believes that members of Congress have more freedom to act on foreign policy issues than on domestic issues. However, it is likely that a wayward Congressman can invoke the wrath of a determined President. Examine the careers of Lodge, Vandenburg, Mansfield, and Fulbright. Is it possible that the prestige of these men insulated them from presidential pressure? What is the plight of the lesser-known Congressman who dissents?
4. The Congress seems to be very interested in the foreign aid program. Why is this issue so closely examined every year? Has foreign aid become the foreign affairs "whipping boy"?
5. Would you propose any changes in the current role of Congress in foreign policy making?

The Politics of the Committees*

Holbert N. Carroll

The House sits, not for serious discussion, but to sanction the conclusions of its Committees as rapidly as possible. It legislates in its committee-rooms; not by the determination of majorities, but by the resolutions of specially-commissioned minorities; so that it is not far from the truth to say that Congress in session is Congress on public exhibition, whilst Congress in its committee-rooms is Congress at work.   Woodrow Wilson[1]

In that happy age of innocence before World War II, the myth persisted that a high wall separated domestic from foreign policy. Participation in a major European war and involvement in scores of minor skirmishes had not yet taught the American people that they had never been as isolated as they supposed. Only one House committee regularly dealt with "foreign affairs." Even this group, so its historian has recorded, was not busy.[2]

The Committee on Foreign Affairs now competes with eighteen other standing committees and miscellaneous select and special units for all the foreign policy business of the House of Representatives. All of these committees are at least indirectly concerned with foreign affairs. More than half of them regularly consider important foreign policy matters, usually in jealous isolation from one another.

Indeed, it is not uncommon for several committees to dabble with one problem. An alert refugee abroad interested in settling somewhere or just in getting fed, for example, should at a mini-

---

*From *The House of Representatives and Foreign Affairs*, Revised Edition, by Holbert N. Carroll. Copyright © 1966, Little, Brown and Company (Inc.) Copyright, 1958, University of Pittsburgh Press. Reprinted by permission of Little, Brown and Company.

[1] *Congressional Government* (New York: Meridian Books, 1956), p. 69. This book was first published in 1885.

[2] Albert C. F. Westphal, *The House Committee on Foreign Affairs* (New York: Columbia University, 1942).

mum keep an eye on the activities of the Committees on Judiciary, Foreign Affairs, and Agriculture as well as several subcommittees of the Committee on Appropriations. It would also pay him to examine stray clauses in bills sponsored by two or three other committees such as Armed Services. Few, if any, Representatives could give a coherent picture of what Congress has provided for assorted refugees, displaced persons, migrants, expellees, and orphans about the globe.

Woodrow Wilson's observations of 1885 are still sound. The House continues to devolve immense powers upon its committees and to serve mainly as a ratifying agency for their decisions. But in 1885, tiny tricklets of legislation flowed from many standing committees to form a small stream of business for the lower chamber. Today, the standing committees and numerous less regular streams pour out an ocean of legislation. The relationship among hundreds of bills is more intimate now than then. Domestic and foreign policy merge into one policy. Military and budgetary considerations impinge upon all areas of policy. Yet the processes of the House for coordinating its control over this vast ocean of business are not much more efficient than in 1885.

To be sure, Congress has periodically reorganized itself. In the reorganization of 1946, strengthened staff services were provided for Congress as a whole, and the committees were encouraged to employ professional staff assistance.[3] The number of standing committees was sharply reduced, and the members of the House, with minor exceptions, were assigned to only one of the new combinations. Committee jurisdictions were broadened and somewhat rationalized in the process.

This modest reorganization helped to improve the quality of legislative control of foreign affairs. Serious deficiencies in the organization and procedures of the House and its committees were not touched, however, and some of the opportunities provided by the act have been but half-heartedly exploited. Only about half of the committees, for example, are well-staffed with competent professional assistance. More important, this reorganization failed to correct the situation ... of divergent and sometimes contradictory committee behavior in foreign affairs. Uncoordinated control of foreign affairs characterizes the behavior

---

[3] P. L. 601, 79th Cong.

of the House of Representatives. Before plunging into this problem of coordination, it is necessary to probe into the anatomy of a congressional committee.

The Anatomy of a Committee

Formal and Efficient Parts

Writers of books on American government generally appreciate the role of committees in the legislative process. The half dozen or so committee decisions required, the resulting decentralization and, in many instances, disintegration of leadership and power, the curious but often tragic consequences of the seniority system, the powerful influence of the committee chairmen, government by a multitude of little governments as Wilson so interestingly described it in 1885 — all of these features have been properly stressed.

The tendency in following this textbook analysis, however, is to look upon committees primarily as institutions, as monolithic bodies of thirty or so men, bodies roughly equal in power and respect in the eyes of the House and men equally attentive to their duties. A committee, to use a distinction made famous by Bagehot in another situation, has its dignified, ornamental, or formal parts and its efficient parts.[4] An appreciation of this distinction, as well as certain other features of congressional committees, is essential for an understanding of the role of these little legislatures in foreign affairs.

The formal part of a committee consists of the chairman and the party majority, a part of the committee which usually sticks together on procedural matters. In short, the formal part of a committee consists of those who in theory supply the initiative and leadership. They may formally approve legislation in the committee and support it with their votes on the floor, but they do little of the real work. On occasion, though, the formal part of a committee may be the efficient part.

---

[4] Walter Bagehot discussed the dignified and efficient parts of English government in *The English Constitution* (World's Classics ed., London: Oxford, 1928).

The efficient part of a committee consists of a core of members, usually only a handful of men representing both political parties. These men actively participate in the hearings, propose the amendments that are accepted, and shape the legislation. They write parts of the committee's report, or at least take the time to slant it to their satisfaction. The efficient element then takes the bill to the floor and fights for it. Their knowledge of the subjects within the committee's jurisdiction may be more specialized than that of the witnesses from the executive branch who appear before them. Department and agency heads and their top assistants are viewed as mere transitory figures by Representatives whose service extends over more than one administration. More than one witness has been confounded by questions and observations drawn from the vast reservoir of knowledge gained by individual Congressmen over decades.

The efficient element of a committee is rarely composed of a majority of the members even though it must carry a majority with it. Probably less than ten members of the thirty-two man Committee on Foreign Affairs, for example, persistently and actively participate in the deliberations of the group. Indeed, in some instances the efficient element may be just one man. This monologic situation is not unknown in subcommittees of the Appropriations Committee, where occasionally just one member has been present to take important testimony to overwhelm his less attentive colleagues.

The efficient part of a committee, moreover, may change from one piece of legislation to another as the interests of the members wax and wane. Each piece of legislation is in a class by itself. The efficient part of a committee, in sum, is the part which wields influence and power. The fruit of its efforts is embodied in statutes and not merely in bills. The men who compose it are the leaders who determine whether the House will play a responsible role in foreign affairs in its committee rooms, on the floor, and in conference committees.

Selection of Members

Chance, modified occasionally by purposeful intrusions by the formal party leaders of the House, determines the quality of a committee's efficient element. Vacancies on committees are formally slated for the Democratic party by the Democrats serving on the Committee on Ways and Means. The Committee on Committees, composed to give representation to the geographical distribution of the party, performs this function for the Republicans. Geography, seniority in the House, the wishes of an applicant, and the desires of the ranking members of the committee with an opening are the major factors weighed when these party agencies slate members for a vacancy.

All of these factors were weighed, for example, when a Democrat from the South serving on the Foreign Affairs Committee was defeated in a primary in 1954. Representatives from the region of the defeated committee member approached Democrats on the Ways and Means Committee to suggest the name of a replacement. The candidate's seniority in the House was adequate for assignment to an important committee. The ranking Democrat on the Foreign Affairs Committee was consulted, and the candidate was informally cleared as satisfactory to the formal party leaders. His foreign policy voting record was checked by some of the more careful Democrats on the Ways and Means Committee. Surviving these tests, the candidate was slated and elected to membership in 1955.[5]

. . . .

Those who slate members for Republican vacancies weigh the same factors as the Democrats, but the Republicans are faced with a greater diversity of foreign policy viewpoints that demand representation. Thus, senior Republicans in the House as a whole, and the party leaders in particular, tend to be more active in slating for vacancies on the foreign policy committee. In 1953, following Eisenhower's election, the two top Republicans of the Foreign Affairs Committee were virtually ignored in the process of filling vacancies on their committee. The Republican leaders of the House made certain that the isolationist element of the party composed about one-fourth of the Republican membership of the committee.

---

[5] This process was described to the writer by a Democrat serving on the Ways and Means Committee.

Unfortunately, the foreign policy views of a Representative, although not always ignored, are not an important factor weighed in the process of filling vacancies on committees other than the foreign policy committee, despite the fact that they handle a large volume of foreign business. Powerful domestic factors enter the picture. Representation on the Agriculture Committee, for example, is not only carefully balanced by regions of the country but also to some extent by crops. The Merchant Marine and Fisheries Committee is liberally packed with Representatives from the major inland and ocean ports of the country. Whether a responsible foreign policy element sits on committees of this sort is thus a matter of chance.

The Environment

From another angle the committees emerge as something more than the bloodless bodies they appear to be in the highly compressed language of the textbooks or even in the hearings and reports. The polished hearings are often artificial and always edited. The real work of a committee is accomplished in executive sessions away from the glare of publicity. The member's public and printed behavior is often different from his private behavior and influence in the very human yet political environment behind locked doors.

Within a committee human beings work together, the majority of them from small town law offices. They frequently do not adequately appreciate the needs and problems of a large bureaucracy. All of them come from single-member districts. They come to the House as individuals, not as players on a team. They often lack the national viewpoint so essential for the responsible consideration of foreign policy matters.

Committees also function in a political atmosphere as do all committee organizations to some degree. Less than one-tenth of the bills debated in Congress arouse intense party controversies, but politics, including the politics of the nation, the states, the local communities, and between the committees, colors all committee action. Grievances and power are much more likely to be vented and exploited at the committee level than at the more disciplined and rule-ridden floor level of the House. Since the decisions of committees normally become the decisions of the House, pressure groups work most avidly at the committee level. To assure proper perspective, it should be mentioned, in addition, that the influence of the committees on the floor of the House varies sharply. Except in times of crisis or when tremendous sums of money are involved, foreign affairs matters bore the members of the House. They sometimes respond with resentment because of the time consumed by such matters. The prestige and influence of the Committee on Foreign Affairs still ranks fairly low in the House. In contrast, some committees, like the Committees on Agriculture and Merchant Marine and Fisheries, have a powerful domestic clientele which they serve with extraordinary bipartisanship. On the floor, they wield tremendous power, sometimes to the detriment of American foreign policy.

Staff

Finally, the staff of a committee must be kept in mind in probing its anatomy. Staff politics is as complex as committee politics. Able professionals, clerks of widely varying competence, some of whom have themselves become institutions, political henchmen of members — all these are scattered among the staffs of the committees of the House of Represntatives. Some of these staff people exert extraordinary influence on policy, and it is not unknown for a zealous staff to capture a committee until the committee amounts to little more than its voice.

To generalize about the staffs of the committees of the House is impossible. In succeeding chapters, the function and role of committee staffs and the performance of particular staffs will be analyzed to determine their impact upon the consideration of foreign policy business in the House of Representatives.

Party Leadership at the Committee Level

An important factor in discussing the politics of the committees in foreign affairs is the role of party leadership. Leadership in the House of Representatives is dispersed. The machinery through which the party leaders work to coordinate party attitudes constitutes only one part, but a significant part, of the leadership picture in the House. The role of the parties and their

leadership at the committee level reflects the well-known loose-
ness of the American party system.

The speaker, the majority floor leader and the chief whip, a
few loyal chairmen, and the majority on the Committee on Rules
compose the key elements in the party picture for the majority.
The minority floor leader and his assistant are the key figures for
the minority party. On some matters, certain other party agencies play a part: a steering committee on occasion; the caucus or
conference rarely and on committee assignments, the Republican Committee on Committees and the Democrats serving on the
Ways and Means Committee. The Democratic leaders rarely
utilize any steering or party policy committee, but the Republican leaders regularly consult with a policy committee composed
of the formal party leaders, the Republicans serving on the Rules
Committee, and ten other Republicans selected on a geographical
basis.

The President keeps in touch through his regular and informal
chats with key Representatives and occasionally, as will be noted
later, through persuasion directed at various groups in stages of
the legislative process. Congressional party machinery, however,
is almost totally divorced from the national party machinery. In
Congress, moreover, there is a meager liaison between the party
leadership of the House and of the Senate.

Although important at other levels of action in the House, the
role of the party leadership is weakest and least significant at the
committee level. The scene might open with the majority floor
leader, whether a Republican or a Democrat, emerging inno-
cently from his office in the Capitol into the middle of a group
of eager reporters. They want his opinion as a party leader on
the action of the Foreign Affairs Committee, let us say, in revis-
ing the foreign aid legislation. The leader will usually hesitate
until the newspapermen indicate by their questioning what the
committee has done. He may then offer a vague comment. This
scene is likely to be repeated in other parts of the building with
different actors, the Speaker and the minority floor leader for
instance. Over at a White House press conference, the President
may be feeling his way through the same fog.

The party leaders are not surprised or even much bothered by
these little scenes. They are not unusual. The substance of even

critical legislation before the committees is strictly committee business, so the tradition runs. Occasionally, a party leader may have advance information as to what a committee intends to do or has done. Otherwise, the leaders, like the public, must depend on the newspapers for their information or perhaps pick up something from people working with the committee on the matter in question. No party leader makes any systematic effort to keep track of committee business and the status of legislation. They have no staffs for these purposes. Their work is almost wholly *ex post facto*. They come into the picture when bills are ready for the floor.

Occasionally, the party leaders may referee disputes between chairmen, conciliate in some other fashion, attempt to blast a bill from committee, and dabble in the selection of committee members. In 1954, for instance, some Republicans from the Foreign Affairs Committee visited the majority floor leader to complain about what they regarded as an intrusion into their jurisdiction by the Agriculture Committee. The farm committee was considering a bill for the disposal of surpluses abroad that was similar to provisions incorporated in bills reported in previous years by the Foreign Affairs Committee. The floor leader was unwilling to do anything to unravel this jurisdictional dispute, and shortly the more powerful Agriculture Committee had its way.

Normally, the party leaders prefer to stay clear of involvement in committee business. Representatives emphasize with pride that the party leaders, the caucus, and the steering committee do not "interfere" with the committees. The theory is that each committee is in charge of a party leader who supposedly looks out for the interest of the party, as worked out with other party leaders and with the responsible executive branch officials, and coordinates his committee's activities with those interests. The ranking minority committee member, in theory performs a similar role for his party.

Committee chairmen wield tremendous power, even if lacking talent and ability. The chairman usually determines what the committee will consider and when; he may control the membership of subcommittees; he is the formal spokesman for the committee to the press and to the executive branch; he is the formal leader on the floor and controls the time and lists of speakers for the majority party in debate; and sometimes he is the man who supplies the appropriate cues to those who desire to know what the executive branch wants. The chairman's role is a dual one. In theory, if not always in fact, he is a party leader, and thus a leader for the Administration if his party is in power. On the other hand, he is the committee chief, and his committee's views may or may not coincide with those of the Administration. A chairman's influence depends a great deal upon his ability to reconcile this dual role.

Is the chairman a party leader? Is he influential? A leader at all? Does he have followers? That depends on the accidents of seniority. His job is the result of his talent in keeping alive and his ability in getting the support of a plurality of less than one-four-hundredth of the nation's voters. No tests of party regularity or of talent are prerequisites for the job.

The seniority system elevates some very capable and influential men to the chairmanships, men who have a sense of party, or at least program, responsibility. Not infrequently, the committee leader may be weak, lacking influence, and unsympathetic with policies supported even by majorities of both parties. Or he may be a strong and influential man with immense retaliatory powers. The Republican victory of 1952, for instance, elevated Representative Daniel A. Reed (R., N. Y.) to the chairmanship of the Ways and Means Committee, a powerful figure generally out of harmony with the foreign trade policy views of the President. And to the chairmanship of the Committee on Foreign Affairs it brought Congressman Robert B. Chiperfield (R., Ill.), a man with an isolationist voting record almost in total opposition to the foreign policy views expressed by the President and other Republican party leaders. Fortunately, Chairman Chiperfield shed his isolationism to support the President in foreign affairs.

Both political parties, in short, like the followers of Adam Smith in economics, operate on the assumption of the natural identity of interests among those who wear the party label. The free enterprise system functions at the committee level. A few of the entrepreneurs, by conviction or otherwise, work with the party leaders.

In committees led by weak chairmen, an "efficient" element

frequently takes over and attempts to work out policy with some attention to party responsibility.

Summary

Ordinarily, a committee is regarded as an institution, as a corporate body with a unitary voice or at most, majority and minority voices. A committee is in a sense an institution. The continuity provided by senior members who pass the biennial political tests, staff people who survive periodic turnovers of personnel, committee tradition, history, and prerogative — all these serve to bind human beings into a collective body. But beneath the surface, a committee is but a few men who make decisions, men who are blessed with no unique capacities beyond those given to other mortals, who deliberate in a very human but intensely political environment, and who, like other men, are sometimes lazy and indifferent, overwhelmed with other business, or devoted to duty.

These committees work in jealous isolation from one another and compete for the foreign policy business of the House. Commonly, the scheme of the separation of powers maintained by checks and balances is discussed in terms of the judiciary, the President, and the Senate and the House. But the House of Representatives is afraid of its own power. A scheme of checks and balances has evolved throughout the House, and especially at the committee level. This scheme is not embodied in a clear theory but is nevertheless part of the fabric of the lower chamber. It aims at preventing the massive accumulation of power and decision anywhere in the House. Facets of the scheme include the weak position of party leaders in dealing with committees, the allotment of business among several committees, many of which work simultaneously and at cross-purposes in the same general area of foreign affairs, and the inheritance of committee leadership according to seniority.

Many other facets mark the sceme. Its ramifications penetrate to the executive branch. It is not uncommon for a congressional committee to develop intimate relations with leading pressure groups and with the agencies of the executive branch in which it has a special interest. The attachment may be sufficiently powerful to defy the best efforts of the President to coordinate and control the executive branch. The Committee on Foreign Affairs, for instance, enjoys a clientele relationship with the Department of State, but the foreign policy viewpoint they support may vary quite sharply from that emerging from another committee in deliberations with its clientele. The combination in foreign affairs may be quite weak in bucking the combination of the Department of Agriculture, farm groups, and the Committee on Agriculture or the combination of the shipping interests, the Maritime Administration, and the Committee on Merchant Marine and Fisheries.

These features of the politics of the committees of the House of Representatives and the effects of these complex relationships in foreign affairs can best be appreciated in the context of specific examples involving major foreign policy areas. . . .

Questions

1. In general, how are members of committees selected? Is it a process you would institute if you were to set up legislative rules of procedure?
2. Does the House Committee on Foreign Affairs enjoy less prestige than its equivalent in the Senate? Why is this so?
3. What is the role of party leadership in the House with respect to foreign policy?
4. The seniority system has been called "the measurement of a man's ability by the length of his beard." Discuss this in terms of the foreign policy process.

Revitalizing the Congressional Role in Foreign Policy

J. W. Fulbright

Senator J. W. Fulbright is the senior senator from Arkansas and is Chairman of the Senate Foreign Relations Committee. He has been sharply critical of American policy toward the Communist world and, particularly, of American involvement in Vietnam. His book *Old Myths and New Reali-*

ties is a collection of some previous speeches on foreign policy. Senator Fulbright asked that the following statement be printed in the Congressional Record, where it appeared on July 31, 1967.

(Statement of Senator J. W. FULBRIGHT before the Subcommittee on Separation of Powers of the Judiciary Committee, July 19, 1967)

In a statement to the Senate Preparedness Subcommittee on August 25, 1966, Secretary of State Rusk said: "No would-be aggressor should suppose that the absence of a defense treaty, Congressional declaration or U.S. military presence grants immunity to aggression." The statement conveys a significant message to any potential aggressor: that under no circumstances could it count on American inaction in the event of an act of aggression. The statement conveys an implicit but no less significant message to the Congress: that, regardless of any action or inaction, approval or disapproval, of any foreign commitment on the part of the Congress, the executive would act as it saw fit in response to any occurrence abroad which it judged to be an act of aggression. It is unlikely that the Secretary consciously intended to assert that Congressional action was irrelevant to American military commitments abroad; it seems more likely that this was merely assumed, taken for granted as a truism of American foreign policy in the 1960's.

I. The Constitutional Imbalance

The authority of Congress in foreign policy has been eroding steadily since 1940, the year of America's emergence as a major and permanent participant in world affairs, and the erosion has created a significant constitutional imbalance. Many if not most of the major decisions of American foreign policy in this era have been executive decisions. Roosevelt's destroyer deal of 1940, for example, under which 50 American ships were given to Great Britain in her hour of peril in exchange for naval bases in the Western Hemisphere, was concluded by executive agreement, ignoring both the treaty power of the Senate and the war power of the Congress, despite the fact that it was a commitment of the greatest importance, an act in violation of the international law of neutrality, an act which, according to Churchill, gave Germany legal cause to declare war on the United States. The major war-time agreements — Quebec, Tehran, Yalta and Potsdam — which, as it turned out, were to form the *de facto* settlement of World War II, were all reached without the formal consent of the Congress. Since World War II the United States has fought two wars without benefit of Congressional declaration and has engaged in numerous small-scale military activities — in the Middle East, for example, in 1958, and in the Congo on several occasions — without meaningful consultation with the Congress.

New devices have been invented which have the appearance but not the reality of Congressional participation in the making of foreign policy. I shall elaborate on these later in my statement and wish at this point only to identify them. One is the joint resolution; another is the Congressional briefing session. Neither is a satisfactory occasion for deliberation or the rendering of advice; both are designed to win consent without advice. Their principal purpose is to put the Congress on record in support of some emergency action at a moment when it would be most difficult to withhold support and, therefore, to spare the executive subsequent controversy or embarrassment.

The cause of the constitutional imbalance is crisis. I do not believe that the executive has willfully usurped the constitutional authority of the Congress; nor do I believe that the Congress has knowingly given away its traditional authority, although some of its members — I among them, I regret to say — have sometimes shown excessive regard for executive freedom of action. In the main, however, it has been circumstance rather than design which has given the executive its great predominance in foreign policy. The circumstance has been crisis, an entire era of crisis in which urgent decisions have been required again and again, decisions of a kind that the Congress is ill-equipped to make with what has been thought to be the requisite speed. The President has the means at his disposal for prompt action; the Congress does not. When the security of the country is endangered, or thought to be endangered, there is a powerful premium on prompt action, and that means executive action. (I might add that I think there have been many occasions when the need of immediate action has been exaggerated, resulting in mistakes which might have been avoided by greater deliberation.)

The question before us is whether and how the constitutional balance can be restored, whether and how the Senate can discharge its *duty* of advice and consent under continuing conditions of crisis. It is improbable that we will soon return to a kind of normalcy in the world, and impossible that the United States will return to its pre-1940 isolation. How then can we in the Congress do what the Constitution does not simply ask of us, but positively requires of us, under precisely the conditions which have resulted in the erosion of our authority? It is not likely that the President, beset as he is with crisis and set upon by conflicting pressures and interests, will take the initiative in curtailing his own freedom of action and restoring Congressional prerogative — that would be too much to expect of him. It is up to the Congress, acting on the well-proven axiom that the Lord helps those who help themselves, to re-evaluate its role and to re-examine its proper responsibilities.

I have the feeling — only a feeling, not yet a conviction — that constitutional change is in the making. It is too soon to tell, but there are signs in the Congress, particularly in the Senate, of a growing awareness of the loss of Congressional power, of growing uneasiness over the extent of executive power, and of a growing willingness to raise questions that a year or so ago might have gone unasked, to challenge decisions that would have gone unchallenged, and to try to distinguish between real emergencies and situations which, for reasons of executive convenience, are only said to be emergencies.

Prior to redefining our responsibilities, it is important for us to distinguish clearly between two kinds of power, that pertaining to the shaping of foreign policy, to its direction and purpose and philosophy, and that pertaining to the day-to-day conduct of foreign policy. The former is the power which the Congress has the duty to discharge, diligently, vigorously and continuously; the latter, by and large calling for specialized skills, is best left to the executive and its administrative arms. The distinction of course is clearer in concept than in reality, and it is hardly possible to participate in the shaping of policy without influencing the way in which it is conducted. Nonetheless, we in the Congress must keep the distinction in mind, acting, to the best of our ability, with energy in matters of national purpose and with restraint in matters of administrative detail.

Our performance in recent years has, unfortunately, been closer to the reverse. We have tended to snoop and pry in matters of detail, interfering in the handling of specific problems in specific places which we happen to chance upon, and, worse still, harrassing individuals in the executive departments, thereby undermining their morale and discouraging the creative initiative which is so essential to a successful foreign policy. At the same time we have resigned from our responsibility in the shaping of policy and the defining of its purposes, submitting too easily to the pressures of crisis, giving away things that are not ours to give: the war power of the Congress, the treaty power of the Senate and the broader advice and consent power.

II. The Legislative Function

Insofar as the Congressional role in foreign policy is discharged through the formal legislative process, the Congress by and large has been able to meet its responsibilities. Unfortunately, however, the area of foreign policy requiring formal legislative action has diminished greatly in recent decades and now contains virtually none of the major questions of war and peace in the nuclear age. Before turning to these critical questions, which go to the heart of the current constitutional crisis, a word is in order about the limited areas of foreign policy which are still governed by the legislative process.

Foreign aid provides the closest thing we have to an annual occasion for a general review of American foreign policy. It provides the opportunity for airing grievances, some having to do with economic development, most of them not, and for the discussion of matters of detail which in many cases would be better left to specialists in the field. It also provides the occasion for a discussion of more fundamental questions, pertaining to America's role in the world, to the areas that fall within and those which exceed its proper responsibilities.

In the last few years the Congress has shown a clear disposition to limit those responsibilities and has written appropriate restrictions, mostly hortatory, into the foreign aid legislation. Only as it has become clear that the executive is disinclined to comply with many of our recommendations has it been found necessary to write binding restrictions into the law. These mandatory restrictions, it is true, impose a degree of rigidity on the executive and constitute a regrettable Congressional incursion on matters of the day-to-day conduct of policy. Here, however, we encounter the overlap in practice between the shaping and conduct of policy and, in order to exert our influence on the one, where it is desirable, we have also had to exert it on the other, where it is not. Were the executive more responsive to our general recommendations — as expressed in committee reports, conditional proscriptions, and general legislative history — it would be possible for us to be more restrained in our specific restrictions.

The matter, at its heart, is one of trust and confidence and of respect of each branch of the government for the prerogatives of the other. When the executive tends to ignore Congressional recommendations, intruding thereby on Congressional prerogative, the result is either a counter-intrusion or the acceptance by the Congress of the loss of its prerogatives. Thus, for example, the persistent refusal of the executive to comply even approximately with Congressional recommendations that it limit the number of countries receiving American foreign aid has caused the Foreign Relations Committee to write numbers into its current bill, proposing thereby to make recommendations into requirements. The price of the flexibility which is valued by the executive is, or certainly ought to be, a high degree of compliance with the intent of Congress.

There are occasions when the legislative process works almost as it ideally should, permitting of the rendering of advice and consent on the matter at hand and also of the formation and expression of the Senate's view on some broader question of the direction of our foreign policy. Such was the case with the test ban treaty in 1963. In the course of three weeks of public hearings and subsequent debate on the floor, the Senate assured itself of the safety of the proposed commitment from a military point of view and at the same time gave its endorsement to the broader policy which has come to be known as "building bridges" to the east. Similarly, the ratification earlier this year of the Soviet consular treaty, which, but for an unexpected controversy might have been treated as routine business, became instead the occasion for a further Senate endorsement of the bridge building policy.

III. Advice and Consent

The focus of the current constitutional problem — one might even say crisis — lies outside of the legislative process, in the great problems of war and peace in the nuclear age. It is in this most critical area of our foreign relations that the Senate, with its own tacit consent, has become largely impotent. The point is best illustrated by concrete examples. Permit me to recall some recent crises and the extremely limited role of the Senate in dealing with them:

At the time of the Cuban missile crisis in October 1962, many of us were in our home states campaigning for re-election. On the basis of press reports and rumors we had a fairly accurate picture of what was happening, but none of us, so far as I know, were given official information until after the Administration had made its policy-decisions. President Kennedy called the Congressional leadership back for a meeting at the White House on Monday, October 22, 1962. The meeting lasted from about 5 p.m. to about 6 p.m.; at 7 p.m. President Kennedy went on national television to announce to the country the decisions which had of course been made before the Congressional leadership were called in. The meeting was not a consultation but a briefing, a kind of courtesy or ceremonial occasion for the leadership of the Congress. At that meeting, the senior Senator from Georgia and I made specific suggestions as to how the crisis might be met; we did so in the belief that we had a responsibility to give the President our best advice on the basis of the limited facts then at our command. With apparent reference to our temerity in expressing our views, Theodore Sorensen in his book on President Kennedy described this occasion as "the only sour note" in an otherwise flawless process of decision making. It is no exaggeration to say that on the one occasion when the world has gone to the very brink of nuclear war — as indeed on the earlier occasion of the Bay of Pigs — the Congress took no part whatever in the shaping of American policy.

The Dominican intervention of April 1965 was decided upon

with a comparable lack of Congressional consultation. Again, the leadership were summoned to the White House, on the afternoon of April 28, 1965, and told that the Marines would be landed in Santo Domingo that night for the express purpose of protecting the lives of American citizens. No one expressed disapproval. Had I known that the real purpose of our intervention was the defeat of the Dominican revolution, as subsequently become clear in the course of extensive hearings before the Senate Foreign Relations Committee, I would most certainly have objected to massive American military intervention.

When, in the wake of the Dominican hearings, I publicly stated my criticisms of American policy, there followed a debate not on the substance of my criticisms but on the appropriateness of my having made them. The question therefore became one of the proper extent and the proper limits on public discussion of controversial matters of foreign policy. The word "consensus" was then in vogue and so extensive had its influence become that there seemed at the time to be a general conviction that any fundamental criticism of American foreign policy was irresponsible if not actually unpatriotic. This was the first of many occasions on which no one questioned the right of dissent but many people had something to say about special circumstances making its use inappropriate. No one, it seems, ever questions the *right* of dissent; it is the *use* of it that is objected to.

I tried at the time of the Dominican controversy to formulate my thoughts on Senatorial responsibility in foreign policy. I recall them here not for purposes of reviving the discussion of those unhappy events but in the hope of contributing to the work of this Subcommittee. I expressed these thoughts in a letter to President Johnson, dated September 16, 1965, and accompanying the speech on the Dominican Republic which I made that day. The letter read in part:

"DEAR MR. PRESIDENT: Enclosed is a copy of a speech that I plan to make in the Senate regarding the crisis in the Dominican Republic. As you know, my Committee has held extensive hearings on the Dominican matter; this speech contains my personal comments and conclusions on the information which was brought forth in the hearings.

"As you will note, I believe that important mistakes were made. I further believe that a public discussion of recent events in the Dominican Republic, even though it brings forth viewpoints which are critical of actions taken by your Administration, will be of long-term benefit in correcting past errors, helping to prevent their repetition in the future, and thereby advancing the broader purposes of your policy in Latin America. It is in the hope of assisting you toward these ends, and for this reason only, that I have prepared my remarks.

"Public — and, I trust, constructive — criticism is one of the services that a Senator is uniquely able to perform. There are many things that members of your Administration, for quite proper reasons of consistency and organization, cannot say, even though it is in the long term interests of the Administration that they be said. A Senator, as you well know, is under no such restriction. It is in the sincere hope of assisting your Administration in this way, and of advancing the objectives of your policy in Latin America, that I offer the enclosed remarks."

I developed these thoughts further in a speech in the Senate on October 22, 1965. It read in part:

". . . I believe that the chairman of the Committee on Foreign Relations has a special obligation to offer the best advice he can on matters of foreign policy; it is an obligation, I believe, which is inherent in the chairmanship, which takes precedence over party loyalty, and which has nothing to do with whether the chairman's views are solicited or desired by people in the executive branch.

". . . I am not impressed with suggestions that I had no right to speak as I did on Santo Domingo. The real question, it seems to me, is whether I had the right not to speak."

Mark Twain said the same thing in plainer words: "It were not best that we should all think alike; it is difference of opinion that makes horseraces."

There are some fundamental and disturbing questions about the way in which we endure controversy in this country, and they go to the heart of the constitutional matters which the Subcommittee is considering. No one objects to a little controversy around the edges of things, to quibblings over detail or to hollow mouthings about morality and purpose provided they are hollow enough.

It is when the controversy gets down to the essence of things, to basic values and specific major actions, to questions of whether our society is healthy or sick, fulfilling its promise or falling short, that our endurance is severely taxed.

Alexis de Tocqueville wrote: "I know of no country in which there is so little independence of mind and real freedom of discussion as in America. Profound changes have occurred since democracy in America first appeared and yet it may be asked whether recognition of the right of dissent has gained substantially in practice as well as in theory." And, as to democracy in general, he wrote ". . . The smallest reproach irritates its sensibility and the slightest joke that has any foundation in truth renders it indignant; from the forms of its language up to the solid virtues of its character, everything must be made the subject of encomium. No writer, whatever be his eminence, can escape paying this tribute of adulation to his fellow citizens." [1]

Until and unless we overcome the disability of intolerance, our democratic processes cannot function in full vigor and as they were intended to function by the framers of the Constitution. The vitality of advice and consent in the Senate is more than a matter of executive-legislative relations. It has to do with our national character and our national attitudes, with our tolerance of deep unorthodoxy as well as of normal dissent, with our attitudes toward the protests of students as well as the criticisms of Senators.

IV. Resolutions and "Consultations"

As I said at the beginning of my statement, two new devices have been invented — more accurately, two old devices have been put to a new use — for the purpose of creating an appearance of Congressional consultation where the substance of it is lacking. I refer to the joint resolution and the Congressional briefing session. Arranged in haste, almost always under the spur of some real or putative emergency, these resolutions and White House briefings serve to hit the Congress when it is down, getting it to

---

[1] Alexis de Tocqueville, *Democracy in America*, Vol. I (New York: Alfred A. Knopf, 1945), p. 265.

sign on the dotted line at exactly the moment when, for reasons of politics or patriotism, it feels it can hardly refuse.

The Gulf of Tonkin resolution, so often cited as an unqualified Congressional endorsement of the war in Vietnam, was adopted on August 7, 1964, only two days after an urgent request from the President. It was adopted after only perfunctory committee hearings and a brief debate with only two Senators dissenting. It was a blank check indeed, authorizing the President to "take all necessary steps including the use of armed force" against whatever he might judge to constitute aggression in southeast Asia.

The error of those of us who piloted this resolution through the Senate with such undeliberate speed was in making a personal judgment when we should have made an institutional judgment. Figuratively speaking, we did not deal with the resolution in terms of what it said and in terms of the power it would vest in the Presidency; we dealt with it in terms of how we thought it would be used by the man who occupied the Presidency. Our judgment turned out to be wrong, but even if it had been right, even if the Administration had applied the resolution in the way we then thought it would, the abridgment of the legislative process and our consent to so sweeping a grant of power was not only a mistake but a failure of responsibility on the part of the Congress. Had we debated the matter for a few days or even for a week or two, the resolution most probably would have been adopted with as many or almost as many votes as it actually got, but there would have been a legislative history to which those of us who disagree with the use to which the resolution has been put could now repair. The fundamental mistake, however, was in the giving away of that which was not ours to give. The war power is vested by the Constitution in the Congress, and if it is to be transferred to the executive, the transfer can be legitimately effected only by constitutional amendment, not by inadvertency of Congress.

The Congress has lost the power to declare war as it was written into the Constitution. It has not been so much unsurped as given away, and it is by no means certain that it will soon be recovered. On February 15, 1848, Abraham Lincoln, then a Member of the House of Representatives, wrote a letter to a man called William H. Herndon, contesting the latter's view that President Polk had been justified in invading Mexico on his own authority because the Mexicans had begun the hostilities. "Allow the President to invade a neighboring nation," wrote Lincoln, "whenever *he* shall deem it necessary to repel an invasion, and you allow him to do so, *whenever he may choose to say* he deems it necessary for such purpose — and you allow him to make war at pleasure. Study to see if you can fix *any limit* to his power in this respect after you have given him so much as you propose."

The Senate, I believe, is becoming aware of the dangers involved in joint resolutions such as the Gulf of Tonkin resolution and earlier resolutions pertaining to Taiwan, Cuba and the Middle East. This awareness was demonstrated by the Senate's refusal to adopt the sweeping resolution pertaining to Latin America requested by the Administration shortly before the meeting of the American presidents at Punta del Este last April. That resolution, which would have committed the Congress in advance to the appropriation of large new sums of money for the Alliance for Progress, was neither urgent nor necessary, it was indeed no more than a convenience and a bargaining lever for the Administration. Its rejection had nothing to do with the Latin American policy of the United States; indeed, it was not the substance of the resolution but the unusual procedure which caused many of us to oppose it. Still less was the rejection of the resolution a matter of "pique" or "frustration," as was alleged by members of the Administration. It was rather a tentative assertion by the Senate that it has come to be doubtful about the granting of blank checks. I hope that it foreshadows further demonstrations on the part of the Congress of a healthy skepticism about hasty responses to contrived emergencies. I hope that it foreshadows a resurrection of continuing debate and of normal deliberative processes in the Senate.

No less defective than the joint resolution as a means of Congressional consultation is the hastily arranged "consultation" — really a briefing — either in committee or at the White House. There is indeed a psychological barrier to effective consultation on the President's own ground. The President is, after all, chief of state as well as head of government and must be treated with the deference and respect due him as chief of state as well as head of government. One does not contradict kings in their palaces or Presidents in the White House with the freedom and facility with which one contradicts the king's ministers in parliament or the President's cabinet members in committee. That indeed is the value and purpose of our Congressional committee system. It permits us to communicate candidly with the President as political leader without becoming entangled in the complications or protocol which surrounds his person. I conclude, therefore, that any meaningful consultation with the Congress must take place on the Congress's own ground, with representatives of the President who can be spoken to in candor and who will speak to us in candor.

They do not always do that, and that is the next problem I would cite. Again and again, representatives of the executive have come before the Foreign Relations Committee to tell us in closed session what we have already read in our morning newspaper. Again and again, they have come not to consult with us but to brief us, to tell us what they propose to do or to try to put a good face on something they have already done. One recent witness devoted a large part of his presentation to an endorsement of the idea of consultation without ever getting around to any actual consulting. At a recent meeting on the Middle Eastern crisis the Administration's witness was unwilling to answer either yes or no to the question of whether he was prepared to assure the Committee that the President would not take the United States into war in the Middle East without the consent of Congress.

Meaningful consultation would consist first of a presentation of provisional views on the part of the Administration and then of a presentation of the views of the members of the Committee, with the Administration witness performing the extremely important function in the second phase of *listening* — listening with an open mind and with an active regard for the fact that, however little he may like it, the men he is listening to are representatives of the people who share with the executive the constitutional responsibility for the making of American foreign policy.

The problem is one of attitudes rather than of formal procedures. The critical question is not whether State Department officials dutifully report Administration acts to Congressional committees or telephone interested Senators to tell them that

American planes are *en route* to the Congo. The question is whether they respond to Congressional directives and recommendations by asking themselves "How can we get around these?" or by asking themselves "How can we carry them out?" The latter, to be sure, can be awkward and irksome for the executive, but that is the kind of system we have. As the political scientist Edwin S. Corwin has written: "The verdict of history in short is that the power to determine the substantive content of American foreign policy is a *divided* power, with the lion's share falling usually to the President, though by no means always." [2] Our legitimate options are to comply with the system or to revise it by the means spelled out in the Constitution but not to circumvent it or subvert it.

"Consultations" which are really only briefings, and resolutions like the Tonkin Gulf resolution, represent no more than a ceremonial role for the Congress. Their purpose is not to elicit the views of Congress but to avoid controversy of the kind President Truman experienced over the Korean War. They are devices therefore not of Congressional consultation but of executive convenience. Insofar as the Congress accepts them as a substitute for real participation, it is an accomplice to a process of illicit constitutional revision.

Some political scientists do not even pretend that there is a role for Congress in the making of foreign policy in the nuclear age. They argue that the authority to declare war has become obsolete and that checks and balances are now provided by diversities of opinion within the executive branch. "This," in the words of the American diplomatic historian Ruhl Bartlett, "is an argument scarcely worthy of small boys, for the issue is not one of advice or influence. It is a question of power, the authority to say that something shall or shall not be done. If the president is restrained only by those whom he appoints and who hold their positions at his pleasure, there is no check at all. What has happened to all intents and purposes, although not in form and words, is the assumption by all recent presidents that their constitutional right to *conduct* foreign relations and to advise the Congress with

---

respect to foreign policy shall be interpreted as the right to *control* foreign relations." [3]

V. Treaties and Commitments

So widespread are American commitments in the world, and so diverse are the methods and sources which are said to make for a commitment, that a great deal of confusion has arisen as to what is required to make a formal commitment to a foreign country. Does it require a treaty ratified with the consent of the Senate? or can it be accomplished by executive agreements? or by simple Presidential declaration? or by a declaration or even a statement made in a press conference by the Secretary of State? The prevailing view seems to be that one is as good as another, that a clause in the transcript of a press conference held by Secretary Dulles in 1957 is as binding on the American Government today as a treaty ratified by the Senate.

If treaties are no more than one of the available means by which the United States can be committed to military action abroad, as Secretary Rusk believes, if the executive is at liberty to commit American military forces abroad in the absence of a treaty obligation as in the case of Vietnam, or in violation of a treaty obligation as in the case of the Dominican Republic, why do we bother with treaties at all? As things now stand, their principal use seems to be the lending of an unusual aura of dignity or solemnity to certain engagements such as the test ban treaty and the outer space treaty.

In addition to the general denigration of treaties, there has developed a widespread attitude, at least on the part of what might be called the foreign policy "establishment," that it is improper for the Senate to reject treaties or attach reservations to them once they have been negotiated. The power of the Senate to accept, reject or amend treaties is of course acknowledged, but it is regarded not as a legitimate function but as a kind of naked power the use of which under any circumstances would be irresponsible. There seems to be a kind of historical memory at

---

[3] Ruhl Jacob Bartlett, *American Foreign Policy: Revolution and Crisis*, Oglethorpe Trustee Lecture Series, Oglethorpe College, Atlanta, Georgia, May 1966, Lecture One, pp. 21–22.

work here; Versailles, like Munich, has conveyed more lessons than were in it.

There appeared in the *New York Times* on March 10, 1967, an interesting and significant editorial commenting on questions that were then being raised in the Senate about the Soviet consular treaty and the outer space treaty. The *Times* commented as follows:

"A treaty is a contract negotiated by the executive branch with the government of one or more other countries. In the process there is normally hard bargaining and the final result usually represents a compromise in which everyone has made concessions. Thus when the Senate adds amendments or reservations to a treaty, it is unilaterally changing the terms of a settled bargain. The practical effect of such action is really to reopen the negotiations and force the other party or parties to re-examine their previously offered approval.

"Every time the Senate exercises this privilege it necessarily casts doubt upon the credibility of the President and his representatives and weakens the bargaining power of the United States in the international arena. The Senate power to do this is unquestioned, but it is equally unquestionable that this power is best used only to express the gravest of concerns, especially in a period of crisis such as is posed by the Vietnam war and efforts to end it."

My attention was arrested by the assertion that a treaty, once negotiated by the executive was a "settled bargain." I had supposed that under our Constitution a treaty was only a *tentative* bargain until ratified with the consent of the Senate.

Returning to my earlier point, the recent crisis in the Middle East reveals the prevailing confusion as to what constitutes a binding obligation on the United States.

In the days preceding the recent Arab–Israeli war there was a good deal of discussion of American responsibilities in the Middle East marked by a prevailing assumption that the United States was "committed" to defend Israel against any act of aggression. As a signatory to the United Nations Charter, which incidentally was ratified by the Senate as a treaty, the United States is indeed obligated to support any action which the United Nations might take in defense of a victim of aggression. The cited sources of the alleged American "commitment," however, were not the United Nations Charter but a series of policy statements, including President Truman's declaration of support for the independence of Israel in 1948, the Anglo–French–American Tripartite Declaration of 1950 pledging opposition to the violation of frontiers or armistice lines by any Middle Eastern state, a statement by President Eisenhower in January 1957 pledging American support for the integrity and independence of Middle Eastern nations, a statement by Secretary of State Dulles in February 1957 stating that the United States regarded the Gulf of Aqaba as an international waterway, a press conference statement in March of 1963 by President Kennedy pledging American opposition to any act of aggression in the Middle East, and a reiteration by President Johnson in February 1964 of American support for the territorial integrity and political independence of all Middle Eastern countries.

The foregoing are all *statements of* policy, not binding commitments in the sense that a treaty ratified by the Senate is a binding commitment. If they were binding and if they were interpreted as requiring the United States to take unilateral action to maintain the territorial integrity of all Middle Eastern states, we would now be obligated forcibly to require Israel to restore all of the territory which she has seized from her Arab neighbors. We are, however, not so obligated. Our only binding commitment in the Middle East is our obligation to support and help implement any action that might be taken by the United Nations. In the absence of such action, we are not bound, not, that is, unless statements in Presidential press conferences are as binding upon the United States as treaties ratified by the Senate.

VI. Restoring Congressional Prerogative

The Foreign Relations Committee has been experimenting in the last two years with methods which it is hoped will help restore the Senate to a significant and responsible role in the making of American foreign policy. Principally, the Committee has made itself available as a public forum for the airing of informed and diverse opinion on both general and specific aspects of American foreign policy. We have invited distinguished professors, scholars, diplomats and military men to talk with the Committee on a wide variety of matters, including the Vietnamese war, American policy toward China, American relations with its European allies, American relations with the Soviet Union and Eastern Europe, and even certain experimental subjects such as the psychological aspect of international relations. In the spring of 1967 the Committee heard testimony by such distinguished persons as George Kennan, Edwin O. Reischauer and Harrison Salisbury in a series of hearings on the "responsibilities of the United States as a global power."

It is by no means clear that public hearings of the kind which have been held in these last two years will prove to be a viable and effective means of bringing Congressional influence to bear on the making of foreign policy. The hearings have been, I emphasize, experimental. They do, however, suggest the possibility of a reinvigorated Senate participating actively and responsibly in the shaping of American foreign policy, in the articulation of the values in which we would have our foreign policy rooted and the purposes which we would have it serve.

I am reasonably confident that the Senate Foreign Relations Committee, by making itself available as a forum of free and wide-ranging discussion, can serve valuable democratic purposes: it can diminish the danger of an irretrievable mistake; it can reduce the likelihood of past mistakes being repeated; it can influence policy both current and future; it can make a case for history and defend America's good name; it can help to expose old myths in the light of new realities; it can provide an institutional forum for dissenters whose dissent might otherwise be disorderly; and, by continuing discussion of crises like the war in Vietnam, it may help us shape the attitudes and insights to avoid another such tragedy in the future.

Free and open discussion has another function, more difficult to define. It is therapy and catharsis for those who are dismayed; it helps to reassert traditional values and to clear the air when it is full of tension. A man must at times protest, not for politics or profit but simply because his sense of decency is offended, because something goes against the grain.

On the Senate floor as well as in the Foreign Relations Committee, vigorous and responsible discussion of our foreign relations is essential both to the shaping of a wise foreign policy and to the sustenance of our constitutional system. The criteria of responsible and constructive debate are restraint in matters of detail and the day-to-day conduct of foreign policy, combined with diligence and energy in discussing the values, direction and purposes of American foreign policy. Just as it is an excess of democracy when Congress is overly aggressive in attempting to supervise the conduct of policy, it is a failure of democracy when it fails to participate actively in determining policy objectives and in the making of significant decisions.

A Senator has the obligation to defend the Senate as an institution by upholding its traditions and prerogatives. A Senator must never forget the Presidency when he is dealing with the President and he must never forget the Senate when he is talking as a Senator. A Senator is not at perfect liberty to think and act as an individual human being; a large part of what he says and what he does must be institutional in nature. Whoever may be President, whatever his policies, however great the confidence they may inspire, it is part of the constitutional trust of a Senator to defend and exercise the advice and consent function of the Senate. It is not his to give away.

Questions

1. In what ways, according to Senator Fulbright, has the Executive usurped congressional power over foreign policy?
2. In introducing his statement, Mr. Fulbright says "It does not respond to any current situation abroad..." (July 31, 1967). Can you accept this as a completely candid statement?
3. Do you agree with Senator Fulbright's analysis? Would your opinion be different if he were not an outspoken critic of the executive branch?
4. What recommendations does Senator Fulbright make to assure effective congressional participation in foreign affairs?

Chapter Four

Coordination of Policy

We have already traced some of the problems created by the constitutional division of powers over foreign affairs between the President and the Congress. A fragmentation of function also characterizes the foreign policy process within the executive branch. The cause of this intrabranch fragmentation is in part the influence of the constitutional system, but fundamentally it stems from the complex nature of foreign policy problems. This complexity determines the nature of the policy-making process, as well as the structure and relationships of the governmental institutions responsible for foreign policy.

Until World War II, the foreign policy process in the United States was almost exclusively the concern of the President and the Department of State. Every effort of other government agencies, including the military, to win recognition of their right to be consulted about foreign policy was rebuffed. Traditionally, foreign policy had not required large sums of money, nor had it needed substantial military forces to make it effective. In those simpler times, war was war and peace was peace; American business had not yet developed large overseas markets; Near Eastern and South American oil was not yet a prize to be protected; and international affairs centered in London, Paris, Vienna, Moscow, and Berlin, not in Washington. Slowly at first, then rapidly during World War II, all of this changed. Once, it was possible to draw sharp lines between peace and war, between domestic and foreign affairs, and between public and private policy; now, these lines are blurred beyond recognition.

As foreign policy problems began to cut across geographical and functional lines, the traditional division of organizational responsibility was called into question, since a single department no longer could assert an exclusive right to make policy. As a consequence, the policy process be-

came one of shared responsibility and overlapping authority. This transformation of the policy process has posed three principal questions: (1)
how to assure efficient and effective operation of the Department of State
as the principal foreign affairs agency; (2) how to relate the problems of
military strategy to foreign policy; and (3) how to coordinate military strategy and foreign policy with strategic and clandestine intelligence activities.

In the re-examination of the State Department, three questions
emerged: (1) should the Department of State be expanded to include all
nonmilitary, foreign policy-related issues and hence to bring them under
one organizational roof; (2) should the emerging aspects of foreign policy
be assigned to newly created organizations; or (3) should existing governmental agencies and departments be permitted to expand their functions
to include foreign policy-related issues. The organizational problems generated by these questions can clearly be seen in the emergence of information and propaganda as a major foreign policy instrument. The first
impulse was to house these activities in the Department of State, but for
a variety of reasons this decision was later reversed, and a new agency
— the United States Information Agency — was created. This same decision
had to be made about foreign aid, intelligence activities, and much of our
financial and economic involvement abroad. The general pattern has been,
not to expand the Department of State, but to solve the organizational
problem by adopting one of the other alternatives. Thus the department has
lost considerable operational control over foreign policy-making which
belies its public image as the sole originator of foreign policy. At best it has
a preferred, not an exclusive, position in the ranks of presidential advisers
on foreign policy.

It is in the context of this reduced operational authority that the discussion of the effectiveness of the Department of State must begin. It is,
of course, popular to criticize the Department for being tradition-bound,
rigid, excessively slow in reaching decisions, and hostile to new ideas.
Criticisms of the Department fall into two general classes. First, there is
that which finds fault with the kind of people employed by the Department
and the Foreign Service. These arguments range from sophisticated
analyses of the organizational style of Department officials to the more
familiar and popular criticisms of them as self-perpetuating, cookie-push-
ing snobs. Politically, the criticisms extend from the rantings of the radical
right about the legacy of Alger Hiss and the secret influence of Communists in the Department to the charges of neo-fascism from the new left.

In each case, the cure is to alter the behavior of the people employed by the Department.

A second group of arguments lays the blame for the inefficiency of the Department of State on the nature of bureaucracy and on the complexity of foreign policy issues. These critics stress the fact that the problems faced by the Department cut across geographical boundaries and functional divisions. Hence, decisions necessarily involve two or more geographical offices as well as two or more functional offices. Decisions in this environment can be reached only after following a complicated clearance process, to assure that all relevant questions have been raised and all material interests consulted. Secretary of State Dean Rusk has spoken eloquently about the problem of "layering" by which he means the number of offices that must be consulted as a decision moves from the bottom of the bureaucracy to the Secretary's desk. The faults of the Department, these critics allege, are those of any large bureaucracy. The able people who serve in the Department and the Foreign Service are victims of the system.

Seen against the complexities of the foreign service policy issues, the Department of State's normal, day-by-day operations do not appear to be less effective than those of other large bureaucracies. If the problems of foreign policy were so simple that they could be handled solely within one geographical or functional office, most of the organizational problems of the State Department would be greatly simplified. Given, however, the nature of the foreign policy process, many criticisms of the State Department reveal less about its ineffectiveness than about the naïve assumptions of the critics. Most criticisms do not mention the Department's own awareness that its normal decision-making procedures are not effective in crises. In serious, but not acute, crises, the Department has hit upon the "task force" as a solution to more rapid decision-making. The task force is a group of officers relieved of their daily duties and assigned to the problem that has created the crisis. This task force then assumes full responsibility within the Department for the solution of the problem. When the crisis subsides, the task force is disbanded, and the problem again becomes the concern of the geographical and functional offices.

The acute crisis calls for a still further modification of the organization. In some cases the Secretary of State assumes direct operational control of the crisis and, in effect, represents, along with a small group of advisers, the entire Department of State. During the Suez crisis of 1956, Secretary of State Dulles by-passed the upper levels of the bureaucracy to deal directly with the crisis at the desk level. Crises, such as the Cuban missile crisis, are so dangerous that policy-making is confined to the presidential level and the Department as an organization does not play an important role in making the decisions, although individual members of the Department may serve as presidential advisers.

No other transformation of the foreign policy process in the United States since 1945 has been given so much thought as the problem of relating military strategy to foreign policy. Out of this concern has grown the concept of a national security policy with diplomatic and military components. The coordination of these two major concerns has had two major expressions. First was the drive to coordinate the armed forces under the Secretary of Defense and Joint Chiefs of Staff. The central purpose of this decision was to provide coordination of military policy and strategy so that there would be only one military voice giving advice to the makers of national security policy

The second thrust was to coordinate military and foreign policy at the presidential level through the use of the National Security Council (NSC). In 1947, when the Council was created, the original concept was that it would be a decision-making body and not just a group of presidential advisers. But the nature of the presidential system of government dictated that no president would be willing to surrender his constitutional power over foreign affairs. Consequently, the NSC has not operated as it was intended. The reasons for this change are clearly explained by Stanley Falk in his article on the NSC. Moreover, except during the Eisenhower administration, the NSC has not had a clearly defined role. President Truman, except for the Korean War period, did not use the National Security Council as a decision-making body; President Eisenhower not only used it as such but gave it a consistent role; President Kennedy disbanded much of the machinery of the NSC system and preferred to achieve the necessary coordination through his Assistant for National Security Affairs, McGeorge Bundy.

The American experience with the NSC shows that under our constitutional system it is impossible for Congress to provide by statute for advisory machinery which the President must use; that presidents have only a limited power to institutionalize decision-making processes and impose these institutional forms upon their successors; and that the NSC did not provide an independent forum where the President could test the advice that the heads of the military and diplomatic establishments gave him. This last point must be stressed, for the NSC was composed of the

very advisers who saw the President in their roles as heads of departments, and therefore it is apparent that the organizational form has not
been a significant factor in assuring the coordination of military and diplomatic elements of national security policy; this coordination occurred,
not because of the NSC, but because in the world of thermonuclear power
there is no way they can be separated.

How to coordinate military strategy and foreign policy with intelligence
(knowledge about other nations, their capabilities and intentions) is the third
question posed by the transformation of the foreign policy process. One
of the traumatic experiences of World War II was the realization that the
United States intelligence services had been totally inadequate. The task
of rectifying this inadequacy became a major order of business after the
war. Since control of the intelligence function was a potential source of
influence over policy, there was no lack of claimants for the task of organizing and directing its revitalization. But the very existence of these conflicting claims meant that none of them could be successful. A new organization, the Central Intelligence Agency (CIA), was created to undertake
the task.

The role of the new agency was to be passive; it was to provide information upon which policy might be based, but it was to eschew any
policy-making role. The National Defense Act of 1947 that created the CIA
also established the Department of Defense, the National Security Council, and the Joint Chiefs of Staff. The act assumed that the various strands of
foreign policy — military, diplomatic, and intelligence — would be strengthened by these organizational changes and would be woven into the finished
fabric through the National Security Council. It was intended that the
military and diplomatic would be the active agents; intelligence would be
the passive member. This model has not been realized in practice because
the expectation that intelligence experts would refrain from entering the
policy arena was unrealistic.

From the beginning CIA has had a dual role: (1) providing the intelligence data required by the decision-makers, and (2) conducting "cloak
and dagger" activities which have clearly had profound policy implications.
The full extent of the policy orientation of this part of CIA functions was
revealed by the investigations following the failure in 1963 of a CIA-
sponsored and -planned invasion of Cuba by a group of refugees. These
investigations showed that the CIA officials, not only planned the invasion,
but originated it and served as its advocate in the policy councils of the
government. This fusing of the intelligence and policy functions is not

necessarily the result of a "plot" by CIA officials to extend their influence but stems primarily from the basic truth in the old saw, "Knowledge is power." This is an almost irresistible tendency on the part of those who know to intrude into the policy process, despite resistance from policy makers. This tendency reflects the fact that the policy-making and the intelligence function are not separate operations. They are parts of a dynamic process and are locked in an inseparable interaction. The expectation that they can be assigned a sphere of action and that sharp demarcation lines can be drawn between them is fully unrealistic. However these functions may be assigned, one must take into consideration the reality that they cannot be isolated from each other.

The history of the past twenty years shows how difficult it is to provide an organizational structure which will give full expression to the complexity of the policy process. Neither the Department of Defense nor the CIA has been able to refrain from usurping, to some extent, the primary foreign policy role of the Department of State. This blurring of roles and functions has resulted, as we have seen, primarily from the nature of the problem, but it has also been influenced by the people who have articulated the roles. During the tenure of Allen Dulles, CIA could operate relatively unfettered, not only because it was effective, but also because Mr. Dulles' brother was the Secretary of State, and both had great influence with President Eisenhower. The Department of Defense has played a significant role in shaping Vietnam policy, not only because that policy requires the use of military force, but also because MacNamara is a forceful Secretary of Defense upon whom President Johnson relies. The Department of State necessarily has had to share its influence over foreign policy with the Department of Defense because foreign policy has become only one component of national security policy, and also because Secretary Rusk is not John Foster Dulles.

The first group of readings in this chapter highlights criticism of the Department of State. Arthur Schlesinger, Jr. is perhaps the most articulate of these critics; the selection, "The Reconstruction of Diplomacy," taken from his book *The Thousand Days,* reflects the feelings of many American liberals. Schlesinger's criticism is responded to by Jack Perry, a Foreign Service officer, who sees much truth in Schlesinger's complaints, but who nonetheless believes that the Department can reform itself.

The two final readings are concerned with the National Security Council and the Central Intelligence Agency. In "The National Security Council under Truman, Eisenhower, and Kennedy," Stanley Falk clearly shows how the National Security Council has been used by various presidents in keeping with their own administrative styles. Harry Howe Ransom, in "CIA: Clandestine Services in an Open Society," is concerned not only with the problems of creating an effective intelligence system, but also with the more fundamental question of the role of that system in a free society.

The Reconstruction of Diplomacy*

Arthur M. Schlesinger, Jr.

Arthur M. Schlesinger, Jr., was special assistant to President Kennedy from 1961 to 1963. He has received two Pulitzer prizes for books: the first, in 1946, for *The Age of Jackson;* the second, in 1965, for his controversial *A Thousand Days: John F. Kennedy in the White House* from which the following selection is taken. He is also the author of *The Vital Center, The Politics of Hope,* and the multivolume work *The Age of Roosevelt.* He has taught American history at Harvard University; he is Albert Schweitzer Professor of Humanities at the City University of New York.

The Institutionalization of Foreign Policy

Kennedy had come to the Presidency determined to make the Department of State the central point, below the Presidency itself, in the conduct of foreign affairs. As Dean Rusk told the Department's policy-making officers a few weeks after the inauguration, there was not "a passive reliance but an active expectation on his part that this Department will in fact take charge of foreign policy." McGeorge Bundy emphasized to the Jackson Subcommittee, which had long been casting a critical eye on the organization of national security policy, that the President wanted no questions to arise concerning "the clear authority and responsi-

*Reprinted with permission, from *A Thousand Days: John F. Kennedy in the White House,* by Arthur M. Schlesinger, Jr., 1965, Houghton Mifflin Company.

bility of the Secretary of State, not only in his own Department, and not only in such large-scale related areas as foreign aid and information policy, but also as the *agent of coordination* in all our major policies toward other nations." [1]

In embarking on this course, Kennedy was influenced not only by a desire to clarify and concentrate the making of foreign policy but also, I believe, by a basic respect for the skills of the Foreign Service. No doubt his attitude toward professional diplomats was mixed. He probably recalled his father's complaints as ambassador to England (Harold Ickes noted in his diary in 1938 that Joe Kennedy "inveighed eloquently against 'the career boys'... insisted that the State Department did not know what was going on ... that nothing got to the President straight unless he sent it to the President direct"). And his visit to Southeast Asia as a young Congressman in 1951 had left him, as he said on his return, with an impression that Foreign Service officers often knew all too little about the nations to which they were accredited, were indifferent to their language and customs, did not represent contemporary America and spent too much time at tennis and cocktails.[2] Nevertheless there were always the Charles Bohlens, Llewellyn Thompsons and Edmund Gullions; and Kennedy's disappointment about the State Department as President sprang in part, I think, from a special sympathy for the diplomatic enterprise. He expected generals and admirals to be refractory and obtuse, but he was not inclined, like Franklin Roosevelt, to write off professional diplomats as inherently stuffy and wrong. In other circumstances he would have liked to be an ambassador himself. He knew that many of 'the career boys' had resented the Dulles regime, and he had looked forward to fruitful collaboration with the Foreign Service and the Department.

The Foreign Service, after all, was the elite unit of the American government. It was in great measure a self-administered body, selecting, assessing and promoting from within. It had deep pride in its *esprit de corps*. "Foreign Service work," as George Kennan wrote, "breeds its own morale, outwardly undemonstrative, often not externally visible, but inwardly far tougher and more devoted

---

[1] My italics.
[2] Meet the Press, December 2, 1951.

than is generally realized." The typical career officer, Kennan continued, was able and patriotic, anxious to learn, to grow in his work and to serve the nation, only too anxious to give loyalty where loyalty was given in return. The process of 'lateral transfer' — the admission to the upper levels of the Service of men trained in other parts of the government — had somewhat diluted the mandarin character of the Service during and after the war; and it entered the postwar world with new accessions of skill and spirit. Anyone who had seen the Service in action well knew the intelligence, decency and selflessness of this group of exceptionally devoted men and women. The White House could always win any battle it chose over the Service; but the prestige and proficiency of the Service limited the number of battles any White House would find it profitable to fight.

Still, as his pre-election task forces reminded Kennedy, the Service had its professional deformations. Moreover, both its vast increase in size and the trauma of the Dulles-McCarthy period had had a disturbing impact on its thought and operation. Thus Adlai Stevenson in his foreign policy report mentioned the "tremendous institutional inertial force" in the Department of State "which, unless manipulated forcefully from the outset, will overwhelm and dictate to the new regime. A similar institutional force in the Defense Department has systematically absorbed a series of Secretaries of Defense." With such comments in mind, Kennedy set up after the election a task force on "State Department Operations Overseas and in Washington." "Even such a distinguished career group as the Foreign Service," the new group soon reported, "has failed to keep pace with the novel and expanding demands of a changing world." The Department had to recognize that "the prototype diplomatic officer of the past, the so-called 'generalist' whose experience was largely 'political,' cannot be the apogee of the Service." Reform, the report conceded, would provoke the cry that the morale of the Service was in danger; but "that raises the question of whose morale? The morale of real concern to the country is that of the young, imaginative, all too frequently circumscribed officer." The task force pointed out that, if Kennedy himself had entered the Foreign Service instead of politics, he could at this point barely qualify for appointment to Class II under existing Foreign Service regulations and would have to wait for seven more years before he could even hope to become a Career Minister.

These strictures emerged from the experience of the years since the Second World War. The role of American diplomacy in prewar days has been largely spectatorial and ceremonial. But in the postwar world our diplomats could no longer be merely observers. They were operators in more than a hundred countries around the planet, and they needed regional knowledge and technical skill as well as personal initiative to make their interventions effective. But in many cases the older career men deplored the new tendencies toward specialization, whether functional or (except for the Russia and China services) regional. They continued to see themselves as gentlemen, not players; the political officer remained the Service's beau ideal. Economic, scientific, cultural, commercial and agricultural attachés made up a rather grubby supporting cast. As for regional expertise, the State Department efficiency report as late as 1963 did not even include the heading "Knowledge of Country and Area," long standard in USIA forms; of seventeen items under "Qualities" not one pertained to area specialization. Younger officers feared that, the better their qualifications for a particular country, the lower rating they would get under "General Usefulness."

Nearly every problem inherent in the Foreign Service process had been compounded by its prodigious growth. In 1930 the Department of State had a budget of about $15 million, the total membership of the Foreign Service was about 1700, and the telegraphic traffic for the whole year amounted to little more than two million words. By the 1960s State had a budget rising toward $300 million, there were over 9000 in the Foreign Service, and every two months the telegraphic traffic was greatest than in all 1930. The Department itself had moved from its pleasant and leisured home beside the White House, with its high ceilings, great fireplaces and swinging doors, to a vast, unlovely building in Foggy Bottom, correctly described by August Heckscher, the President's Special Consultant on the Arts, as a "monument to false functionalism and false grandeur."

As it grew in size, the Department diminished in usefulness. This was in part the consequence of bureaucratization. 'Layering' — the bureaucrat's term for the imposition of one level of ad-

ministrative responsibility on top of another — created a system
of 'concurrences,' which required every proposal to run a hope-
lessly intricate obstacle course before it could become policy.
Obviously clearance was necessary to avoid anarchy, but it often
became an excuse for doing as little as possible. The mounting
unwieldiness of the procedures drove Kennan to the gloomy conclusion that, in really delicate and urgent situations, "American
statesmen will have to take refuge in a bypassing of the regular
machinery and in the creation of ad hoc devices — kitchen cab-
inets, personal envoys, foreign offices within foreign offices, and
personal diplomacy — to assure the intimacy of association, the
speed, the privacy, and the expression of personal style essential
to any effective diplomacy."

Franklin Roosevelt and Cordell Hull had started the Department's descent from its traditional place at the summit of the
foreign policy process — Roosevelt because he wanted certain
things done and Hull because he was not temperamentally able to
do them. Thwarted in the Secretary's office, Roosevelt fell into
the habit of using other instruments — first Sumner Welles, the
Under Secretary; then other Cabinet members, like Secretary of
the Treasury Henry Morgenthau, Jr.; and later General George
C. Marshall and the Joint Chiefs of Staff, new agencies such as the
Office of War Information and the Board of Economic Warfare,
and personal envoys, like Harry Hopkins and Averell Harriman.
No Secretary of State after the war, not even Acheson or Dulles,
was quite able to gather back the vanished powers. By 1961 the
State Department was but one of many bodies involved in foreign
affairs. The London Embassy, for example, housed representatives of forty-four agencies of the United States government.

Bureaucratization was only part of the explanation for State's
malaise when Kennedy came to office. The other part was the shock
of McCarthy — or rather the shock of the readiness of Dulles, as
Secretary of State, to yield up Foreign Service officers to Mc-
Carthyism. The Dulles period was a time of distress and humilia-
tion for the professionals. These years saw the expulsion of experienced and independent-minded diplomats, like John Davies,
Jr., and the exile of others, like Charles Bohlen. A proud Service
found itself ordered about by Scott McLeod, a coarse straw boss
whom Dulles brought in as Security Administrator, and cowering

before juvenile comedians like Roy Cohn and G. David Schine. Circumspection had always eased the path to advancement in the Service; now it became a requirement for survival. The McCarthy era, by demonstrating the peril of dangerous thoughts, elevated conformism into a conditioned reflex. Career men stopped telling Washington what they really thought and consecrated themselves to the clichés of the cold war. Some did this more skillfully than others, and the result, as Davies wrote later, was that "many cautious mediocrities rose to the top of the Service," along with those most uncritically committed to the cold-war view of the world.

.   .   .   .

Foggy Bottom in 1961

This was the situation which confronted Kennedy in his attempt to make the Department the agent of coordination.

The new administration almost immediately bogged down in the bureaucratic tangle. Men like Harriman and Kennan, who had known the Department as late as the Truman administration, were startled by the transformation of a decade. When a foreign ambassador made a courtesy call on Harriman early in 1961, a junior officer mysteriously appeared to record the conversation. Harriman ascertained that he planned to write an *aide-mémoire,* submit it to Harriman for correction and send copies to all interested bureaus and embassies, where presumably it would have to be read, pondered and filed. Shuddering at the proliferation of paper and the expenditure of energy, Harriman said that, if by chance anything of consequence were said, he would inform somebody and told the officer to go away.

The machinery was becoming an end in itself. Dean Rusk remarked to the Jackson National Security Subcommittee that he often read in the morning telegrams specific questions to which he knew the specific answer, but each telegram would nonetheless have to go "on its appointed course into the Bureau, and through the office and down to the desk. If it doesn't go down there, somebody feels that he is being deprived of his participation in a matter of his responsibility. Then it goes from the action officer back up through the Department to me a week or ten days later, and if it isn't the answer that I knew had to be the answer, then I [have to] change it." (We experienced the results with some exasperation at the other end of the White House line. The Department had the habit of sending cables over at the end of the day and demanding immediate presidential clearance in the most urgent terms, when we knew that the document had probably taken three weeks to move from the country desk into and out of the top offices on the seventh floor.) And all this involved more than just the waste of time. "The heart of the bureaucratic problem," Rusk once observed, "is the inclination to avoid responsibility." The President used to divert himself with the dream of establishing a secret office of thirty people or so to run foreign policy while maintaining the State Department as a façade in which people might contentedly carry papers from bureau to bureau.

.   .   .   .

The Uneasy Partnership

Yet, in spite of the presidential effort to give the Department the central role in foreign affairs, Richard Neustadt was obliged to testify before the Jackson Subcommittee in 1963: "So for as I can judge, the State Department has not yet found means to take the proffered role and play it vigorously across the board."

Part of the trouble was inherent in the effort, as Neustadt defined it, to make the State Department "at once a department and then something more." The Secretary already had, in the jargon, a 'full plate.' He had to manage and represent the Department and Foreign Service, attend to Congress and public opinion and take part in conferences and negotiations all over the planet. To do all this and serve in addition as the President's agent of coordination would require almost superhuman talent and energy. It was not that the Department failed to produce statements of plans and objectives. If anything, it produced too many — a Basic National Security Program, State Department guidelines, country plans, internal defense plans, national policy papers and so on. But the process of codification tended toward generalization and ambiguity and rarely provided specific guidance on the hard choices.

Part of the trouble too lay in the attitude of the White House toward the Foreign Service. Talk of the need for specialization was all very well; but, as Charles Bohlen used to urge with urbane persuasiveness, the art of diplomacy must also be recognized as a specialization and basic to the others. It was Bohlen who, among Foreign Service officers, saw most of Kennedy in the relaxed moments of his Presidency. The gaiety of Bohlen's mind, the shrewdness of his insight, and the breadth of his experience made him a delightful companion. At the same time, though he was infinitely more independent and irreverent than the typical career officer, the Foreign Service had no more faithful or ingenious champion. Once Kennedy, exasperated over the difficulty of getting action out of State, said, "What's wrong with that goddamned Department of yours, Chip?" Bohlen answered candidly, "You are."

By this Bohlen meant, as he explained to an interested Kennedy, that the President did not make sufficient allowance for the virtues of professionalism. He wanted quick and personal replies to significant questions, not taking into account the fact that any significant question had a bundle of implications which the Department must consider in an orderly way before it could make a responsible answer. He wanted ambassadors to know languages, master technical fields and fraternize with the people of the countries to which they were assigned, forgetting that the chief purpose of the diplomat was the transaction of business between governments and that everything else was supporting and subsidiary. Too much emphasis on diplomatic activism per se might lead people to forget the limits of diplomatic action. Bohlen even argued that the Assistant Secretaryships should be filled from the Service, though, when Kennedy mildly observed that it was not easy to find good Foreign Service officers, Bohlen conceded that this was so.

The aggressiveness of the White House staff no doubt compounded the trouble. Probably most of the Foreign Service had welcomed Kennedy's accession. Yet a year later many career men were wondering whether they had not exchanged King Log for King Stork. White House 'meddling' struck some of the pros as careless intrusion by impulsive and ignorant amateurs — "crusading activism touched with naïveté." This was John Davies's phrase, and he added: "Bold new ideas and quick decisions were asked of men who had learned from long, disillusioning experience that there were few or no new ideas, bold or otherwise, that would solidly produce the dramatic changes then sought, and whose experience for a decade had been that bold ideas and actions were personally dangerous and could lead to congressional investigations and public disgrace." In his visits to Washington, Davies would talk acidly about the Foreign Service, "purged from the right under Dulles, now purged from the left under Kennedy," and ask, "How can you expect these men to do a good job?"

The question was a real one. The Foreign Service obviously had to carry out the policies of the administration; yet 'thought correction,' even in favor of the New Frontier, presented its problems. The President, commenting on the public service in his first State of the Union message, had said, "Let it be clear that this Administration recognizes the value of dissent and daring — that we greet healthy controversy as the hallmark of healthy change." But what if dissent meant opposition to the neutralization of Laos or to the Alliance for Progress or to the center-left experiment in Italy? This was a riddle which the White House, wishing free minds in the bureaucracy but at the same time demanding commitment to its policies — and the Foreign Service, proclaiming its loyalty to all administrations but at the same time reserving the right to defend old policies against new — never solved. Probably it was insoluble.

These structural factors explained part of the State Department's faltering response to its "proffered role." The partnership seemed chronically out of balance. But Kennedy never ceased hoping that it would work. He tried one thing after another. "I have discovered finally that the best way to deal with State," he said to me one day in August, 1961, "is to send over memos. They can forget phone conversations, but a memorandum is something which, by their system, has to be answered. So let's put as many things as possible in memoranda from now on." Though he licensed an exceptional degree of White House interest in foreign policy, he set up no new authorities which would prevent the Secretary of State from serving as the presidential 'agent of coordination.' Instead, he repressed his frustrations (at some times more successfully than at others) and kept supposing that by strengthening the direction of the Department he would enable it to sustain its side of the partnership.

Questions

1. Professor Schlesinger's criticisms seem to be directed against certain conservative social and political attitudes in the Department of State. The author is a self-professed "liberal." Is there a connection? Do Schlesinger's remarks have less meaning in the light of his political views?
2. Does the author believe that the attitudes of the Foreign Service work to the disadvantage of good foreign policy-making? Is he really just uttering traditional criticisms of bureaucratic inefficiency?
3. What is "layering" in the Department of State? How does it affect the foreign policy process? Make a qualitative judgment.
4. Refer to Jack Perry's article in this book. How does he react to Schlesinger?

Sorensen and Schlesinger and the Service*

Jack Perry

Jack Perry, a former journalist, is a Foreign Service officer in the United States Department of State. Educated at Mercer University and the Russian Institute at Columbia University, Mr. Perry presently is serving as political officer in the United States Embassy, Paris.

This is not a book review. All we need say about these familiar books as reading matter is that surely every Foreign Service officer interested in foreign policy will want to read them.

This is also not a rejoinder to criticism. Some of Schlesinger's opinions, especially those about particular people, I consider unfair or false; but that is not the point under consideration here.

*Reprinted from *Foreign Service Journal*, May 1966, by permission of the American Foreign Service Association.

Sorensen and Schlesinger offer us a serious examination of the functioning of American diplomacy as it looked from the White House. We are given the rare opportunity to see ourselves as the President's staff saw us only yesterday. As for the criticism, of which there is considerable, I see no profit in rebuttal. The sensible course is to examine their examination of us and learn what they have to teach — to *make* the criticism constructive no matter how it was intended.

What I want to do is identify the major points of criticism, separate the grave from the merely worrisome, and hopefully invite others to derive and apply the lessons.

. . . .

How did we do? Gritting our teeth, let us quote a few epithets: "bowl of jelly," "tradition ridden bureaucracy," "built-in inertia which deadened initiative," "tendency towards excessive delay," "bureaucratic patois," "professional deformations," "a zone, or climate, of inertia," "full, ripe dreariness of utterance," "conspiracy of the conventional against the unconventional," "formless and impenetrable," "cold-war view of the world," "intellectual exhaustion," "those people over there who are constantly smiling." The drift seems clear enough.

Are some of our faults endemic to diplomacy? Being at NATO, where communicative diplomats abound, I asked several, "What are the weaknesses of *your* Foreign Service and Foreign Ministry?"

We do share certain vulnerabilities. European diplomats are often called unrepresentative, for example, just as Kennedy said (in 1951) that Foreign Service officers "did not represent contemporary America." . . . The old-versus-young problem is shared — the difficulties the "young, imaginative and circumscribed" (as a Kennedy task force report put it) encounter in being heard and in getting ahead. This is part of being humans in groups, but in our business it sometimes has special overtones of caution and conservatism versus vigor and liberality. All Foreign Offices share the problem of making the organization correspond to the demands upon it, and organization-chart rheumatism is a common ailment — although, as noted below, we Americans seem to have direr problems than anyone else. What we share most of all, however, is diplomacy's inherent leave-well-enough-alone tendency. All diplomats are aware of the restraints imposed by the fact that other countries too have power, problems, and foreign policies. We are all prone to a tendency to live with problems rather than attack them, to muddle rather than to meddle.

Other Services have some problems we do not. For example, to get into and succeed in many diplomatic services, you must still be of a certain family or a certain background. Our Service has broadened its range — class, educational, racial, and geographical — without too great sacrifice of merit; and this is laudable. Moreover, in many services — Old World, Communist, or Third World — there persists a more rigid hierarchy of the superior in rank over the inferior, and a concomitant suspicion that inferiors do not work unless goaded: this engenders a stiffness, a spurring-on, a ruthlessness, that is rare with us. We should take pride in our relaxed equality and in our habit of working at capacity without being prodded.

But other weaknesses are especially American. Difficulties in handling our own language, for example (not to mention foreign ones). Or the problem of numbers, being lost among multitudes of colleagues (when I asked one NATO associate his idea of American diplomatic short-comings, his immediate comment was, "You seem to have an extraordinary number of people."). Difficulty in coordinating foreign policy among competing agencies also seems to be peculiarly American. . . . And in the bowl of jelly department, our problems soar above other nations: owing to many special circumstances — our country's standing, our bureaucracy's size, our tradition of tinkering with the machinery, our fluctuations in foreign policy — we seem to have a harder time making our collective diplomats efficient and responsive. . . .

Finally, responsibilities for foreign *policy* vary greatly. Most Foreign Ministries, especially those under the cabinet system, expect the Minister to make policy, and he expects his Ministry to carry it out. The Minister is on the spot politically more than our Secretary of State — which is saying something — but his Ministry is more insulated from politics than our Department is. (In some Foreign Ministries attempts to initiate policy, or even influence it too much, mean career suicide or exile. Others — for example the British — have policy-making problems much more

like ours.) But in general, foreign diplomats are less exposed than
we are to the kitchen heat. This is a ponderable point.

. . . .

On to the criticism! . . .

1. *Poor English:* "the poverty of the official rhetoric." Schlesinger hits hard on this. With some praiseworthy exceptions,
shall we not plead guilty? Perhaps the root fault is in our American idea of education; the fact stands that we in the Service
turn out poor English too often. All the Service can do, in my
opinion, is to be more stringent about admitting only those who
know a little English, and to be far more rigorous in setting and
demanding high prose standards. Writing well is a habit, a discipline, an atmosphere, a process of emulation, as the French
diplomatic service illustrates: let us begin.

2. *Lack of Control of Foreign Affairs.* Guilty but with ex-
tenuating circumstances? Certainly becoming the "agent for coordination" of the two trans-Potomac power-houses is a Her-
culean undertaking — not to mention our other friendly rivals.
But in some ways, since FDR, we have made noteworthy progress.
A great change in postwar American diplomacy, for example, is
the improvement in cooperation between Executive and Legislative; and the Department's contribution, by vastly bettering its
own relations with the Hill, is not given enough credit. Coordination overseas, in the Embassies, is improving, it seems. And on
the lower levels, where our cross-fertilization exchange programs
are in effect with Defense, Treasury, and so on, a solid basis for
understanding is being built.

At bottom, of course, size and complexity are the enemies,
and each President will approach foreign policy coordination
differently. All we officers can do, perhaps, is learn as much about
the other agencies as possible, take their points of view into account in our foreign policy thinking, and give the Secretary the
best support we can. Within certain limits I believe we can assure
State's predominance — and I am convinced State ought to be pre-
dominant — if we show each new Administration that we have the
best men and the best ideas. But that is not easy, and no doubt this
American problem will stay with us.

3. *Conservatism, Anti-Liberalism.* Although I knew that

Schlesinger was somewhat to the left of David Lawrence, I was sincerely taken aback at his hammering on this point. We are supposed to have a "cold-war view of the world," to harass Latin American liberals, to oppose Italy's "opening to the left," to place corporate investments before social progress, to sustain reactionary regimes wherever we can, and so on. Above all, we are supposed to be obsessed with a monolithic monster that we persist in calling, despite Schlesinger's instructions, the "Sino-Soviet bloc." Either Schlesinger or I, it seems, has too selective a view of the Service. I have been in the Soviet area since early 1960, for example, and I do not know anyone involved in Communist affairs in the Service who thinks in terms of a monolithic "Sino-Soviet bloc." Neither do I know any anti-liberals, or neo-colonialists, or Birchers. My personal impression after six years is that most Foreign Service officers are non-doctrinaire progressives, and that the Service and Department in general do not approach foreign policy problems in terms of ideology — although we take it into account. Certainly we have some conservatives — if we are to be representative of America, we had better keep some, had we not? — but I feel our collective outlook is practical and moderately liberal. I do not see conservatism as a major long-range problem for us. Am I wrong?

4. *Foreign Policy Shortcomings.* Schlesinger quotes Theodore H. White that we were "almost unfit for any policy-making purpose or decision." As noted above, most Foreign Ministries have drastically circumscribed roles in policy formulation. I am not certain how far our own mandate runs. If my lack of certainty is because I am below the policy-making level, which I certainly am, then fine; but if it is also because Sorensen and Schlesinger share my lack of certainty, which I think they do, then there is more room for disquiet.

. . . .

Of course the question of who makes policy, and how, is one that the boys on the political science quarterlies, as A. J. Liebling used to say, play around with a lot. White House staffers probably dream about receiving a stream of fresh, firm, incisive ideas that they can pass up for conversion through Presidential alchemy into Foreign Policy. In real life the process is much more complex and messy. When the Department goes too far in trying to make policy itself, the White House says we are cautious and frozen. There is probably a pendulum effect, too, and we are especially vulnerable when push-on administrations follow pull-back ones....

. . . .

Is it not true that, given the complexity of foreign policy-making nowadays, given Wristonization and the presence of Foreign Service officers in many agencies at all levels, *most* American diplomats above a certain rank are going to be intimately involved in foreign policy-making whether they want to be or not? This was not true for Nicolson, who divided the popular concept of "diplomacy" into two parts, "the management of international relations by negotiation," true diplomacy, which diplomatists did, and "foreign policy," which Ministers did. This division is still valid in many countries. But at least in our country the line between policy-maker and policy implementer has become very hard to draw, and most Foreign Service officers find themselves on both sides of the line successively or simultaneously. This is a new dimension in our careers, and it deserves study.

5. *Inefficient Organization,* "the bowl of jelly." This is the weakness most lambasted in both books. The White House was disappointed in our lack of vigor and the difficulty in making us a "mechanism for swift information and decision."

Certain reasons are adduced: FDR's mistrust of State, the sudden post-war proliferation of responsibilities, the shocks of the McCarthy era, our vast increase in numbers. But basically, I feel, Sorensen and Schlesinger, who respected many of us as individuals, were genuinely puzzled as to why collectively, in an outfit as comparatively small as ours, we could not rev up and crank out a better product more quickly.

Personally, I am puzzled too. Judging by my own observations, as individuals we work hard and fast — generally harder and faster than all but a few foreign diplomats — and we have superb tools to work with. But when you lump us all together, and bid us work fast, mystifying problems develop.

Certainly we have made many steps forward recently. We all recognize that weight of numbers still hurts our efforts. Most of all, we know that the complexity of American foreign policy today makes inevitable some tangle in the organization charts, some slowness, some gelatination. You can still wreck a foreign policy by failing to clear one telegram, alas, and you cannot put a deadline on things like a non-proliferation treaty or NATO nuclear sharing because the patient will not respond to shock treatment. But when all this is said, I for one still have this intestinal emotion that we are too big and too fat and too slow. Am I wrong?

6. *Caution, Conventionality, Rigidity:* "The hardest thing of all was to change anything." This is linked with our organizational troubles, but separable; here our authors are talking about a disease of the Departmental mind. Schlesinger says the Service takes independent-minded young men and squeezes the independence out of them, making one definition of a Foreign Service officer "a man for whom the risks always outweighed the opportunities."

Now this is a nubbly one. As discussed above, the leave-well-enough-alone syndrome is part of diplomacy — awareness of limitations, sensitivity to objection, the inherent superficiality of a jack-of-all-trades profession.

What is more, censure of our caution is often an expression of temporary government looking askance at permanent government. . . . The memoirists may vivisect our foreign policy and examine still quivering segments labeled "GOP Years," or "JFK Era," but we work daily with the subject of their experiments and must treat the patient as a living whole. One may argue that, within bounds, restraint and even caution are beneficial, especially in a time when survival itself is wagered and policies, as Neustadt observed, tend to became "irreversible." And State is probably the normal place for this diplomatic caution to be institutionalized within the permanent government, for Defense and CIA are more "activist" than we are, generally speaking, because of the nature of their responsibilities.

But once again, I myself could not in all honesty deny the charge. The pressures towards conformity, towards not being wrong, are still very grêat, and we still err more often on the side of timidity than of *trop de zèle*. Our best men are forthright and courageous, but many of us, finding courage discouraged, fail to stand forth. Am I wrong? This is the criticism that I found most telling.

If we take Sorensen and Schlesinger seriously, we ought to be talking to each other about our shortcomings and how to overcome them. I will try to play gadfly.

Some shortcomings are inherent. Like other diplomats, we will embody a certain amount of diplomatic reserve and caution, and our organization will reflect this. As permanent government, we will cause stress and invite criticism when we stand for continuity in policy as against the innovations of each new administration. The dilemma of making too much policy or not enough will remain. Defense and CIA will not wither away — nor will the White House Staff, of course. And the personal relationship of the President and his Secretary of State will continue to underlie everything else, no matter what we bureaucrats do.

But surely there are things we can do. I now indulge in what a NATO diplomat — not from an English-speaking country — called "loud thinking."

1. *Man over Machinery.* At a certain level we have learned, or ought to have, that tinkering with the machinery does not solve the problem: setting up an OCB does not guarantee coordination. This basic verity is true for our Department too, most of us recognize; but we still seem to be more concerned with the organization than the men in it. Many of us feel ourselves getting more and more lost in the machinery.

Are we too big to aim at a man-directed, man-serving machine? Instead of improving the machine, can we find ways to get better men? Instead of molding us to fit the machinery, can they mold it to fit us?

For example: Avoid making us numbers. Stop using the A-100 course to produce new little bureaucrats. Quit trying to categorize and specialize us and let us be ourselves, as broad or as narrow as we can make ourselves. Drop the junior officer rotation program and let new men do real work. Do not career-plan us and round us off so much that the individuality is taken away: let each career be unique. Get rid of some of us and give the rest more to do. Admit that understanding foreign policy is a full-time job, and let no one waste his time on made-work or on housekeeping. Could we try harder to clear away all the debris and just work?

2. *Standards of Excellence.* If the President expects us to excel, we should try harder for excellence. Being broad and representative does not have to mean mediocre.

To be very frank, we make little attempt to set high standards. ... From the building we are housed in to the posters on its walls, from our Administrative Memoranda to our top secret telegrams, from the *Newsletter* to the *Journal,* we work in an atmosphere where mediocrity is tolerated and above-average is not demanded. We approach the point where file clerks will be considered more important than political counselors because they are more numerous. For good reasons — who opposes money? — we have joined forces with the mailmen and are advancing on a broad front towards equality with industry. Is that our goal? I accept my paycheck meekly, but I am bold enough to say that no good American diplomat of my acquaintance became one for the pay. And I have yet to meet a good one who resigned for lack of pay, although some of the best I knew resigned because they were given no work to do equal to their abilities. We may work harder than most other diplomats, but we do not demand enough of ourselves.

Why can we not impose standards of excellence and insist they be met?

3. *Encouraging Courage.* We cannot respect our leadership enough for the courage it has shown in recent years in standing stoutly by us: we must return the compliment by being courageous.

Since I joined the Service I have learned, to my own satisfaction at least, that being a good diplomat means exercising good judgment. Judging requires courage, for every judgment is a reputation wagered. I am full of admiration for our best men, who have this capacity and this courage in abundance and who exercise it daily. But as an organization, we still put the premium on not being wrong; collectively we tend to flee judgment and to substitute re-examination, postponement or decision by committee.

We should penalize not for judging wrong but for refusing to judge. We should encourage courage.

This cuts deep. Courage is required in many houses if we are to speak out bravely about the necessity of birth control, the persistence of Peking or Havana, the priority of the public sector, the missing prerequisites for democracy or economic growth, the realities of a polycentric world, and on and on. Schlesinger thought us reactionary, and some future administration's historian might think us radical: if we are to serve as we should, we need the courage to be what we must be, regardless.

But men of courage tend to be mavericks, non-conformists, trouble-makers. Are we brave enough to put up with them and let them be what they are?

4. *Thinking Like the President*. If we have indeed gone beyond Nicolson's definition and are in the sticky situation where foreign policy-making is all bound up at every level with policy-execution, then our thinking about foreign affairs must be as broad as the President's.

I see big holes in my own argument. We are not expert enough, we are not up for election, we are not close enough to the Hill, we dilute our effect when we mix in political thinking, and so on. But if Sorensen and Schlesinger are right, the root trouble, under all the "jelly" and "inertia" and the rest, was our failure to think about foreign policy the way Kennedy did.

I do not mean, of course, that we should try to anticipate what the President will think. We should tell him what *we* think is right, in terms of reference as broad as his; and then let him decide if we are right or wrong. I know this is already done on the highest levels. But if we could *all* do that, the whole Service, the whole Department, then we could attain foreign policy coordination by leadership rather than by combat. (There would be no further need to seek coordination by absorption, as with USIA officers; obviously Defense and CIA are indigestible anyway.) If we could do that, we would not need to talk about being an elite, for we would be one.

In order to think collectively on as broad a plane as the President, we would have to leave our best men free to think individually. We would have to adapt our organization to their needs instead of vice versa. We would have to set high standards, and give special treatment to those who met them. And we would have to have the courage to support these men, these ideas, these standards. This is the kind of Service the President wants and the country needs.

At least those are the first thoughts, no doubt naïve, that

Sorensen and Schlesinger arouse in one Service reader. Am I wrong?

Questions

1. Mr. Perry has a vested interest in the Foreign Service. Do you think his review of the two books is objective?
2. Discuss Perry's reaction to each of the major areas of criticism.
3. What is Perry's concept of "permanent government"? Do you agree with him?

The National Security Council under Truman, Eisenhower, and Kennedy*

Stanley L. Falk

Stanley L. Falk, Associate Professor of National Security Affairs at the Industrial College of the Armed Forces in Washington, D.C., is the author of *Bataan: The March of Death* and *Decisions at Leyte*. After serving from 1945 to 1948 as an intelligence and historical officer in the Far East with the armed forces, Dr. Falk returned to Washington to work in the Office of Military History, Joint Chiefs of Staff, where, from 1959 to 1962, he was Senior Historian.

The National Security Council, in the words of one observer, "constitutes the most ambitious effort yet made to coordinate policy on the cabinet level in the American federal government." [1] Created by the National Security Act of 1947 and subsequently modified or expanded by Congress and the President, it represents an attempt to fill a long-recognized need for a single, top-ranking

*This study was originally prepared in slightly different form for use by students of the Industrial College of the Armed Forces, Washington, D.C. In its present form, it appeared in *Political Science Quarterly*, September, 1964, Vol. LXXIX, No. 3. Permission has been granted to reprint it here with some omissions.

[1] Paul Y. Hammond, "The National Security Council as a Device for Interdepartmental Coordination: An Interpretation and Appraisal," *American Political Science Review*, LIV (1960), 899.

body to formulate and correlate national policy. Its roots lay in the British Committee of Imperial Defense, a Cabinet agency for coordinating national security matters, and in certain American attempts to provide a similar mechanism. The American efforts dated back to World War I but took form most notably in the Standing Liaison Committee of the early nineteen-forties and the State-War-Navy Coordinating Committee established in 1944.[2]

Yet the Committee of Imperial Defense was an arrangement more suited to Cabinet than to presidential government, and none of the American examples was extensive or effective enough to solve the pressing problems of policy formulation and direction that arose in the hectic days following World War II. It was at the height of the postwar unification struggle, then, that Ferdinand Eberstadt, in a study prepared for Navy Secretary James Forrestal, urged the establishment of a National Security Council as "a policy-forming and advisory" body of top government officials to assist the President in making and coordinating "overall policies in the political and military fields." [3]

The National Security Act of 1947 accepted the Eberstadt recommendations for the establishment of the NSC. The Act created a Council consisting of the President, who would chair its meetings or, in his absence, designate another member to do so; the Secretaries of State, Defense, and the three Services; the Chairman, National Security Resources Board; and certain other officials whom the President, if he wished, might designate with the advice and consent of the Senate. A permanent staff would support the Council.

The function of the NSC, briefly stated, would be to assist the President in integrating and implementing national security policy. Specifically, the Council would examine American national security goals in relation to national power, study policies on areas of common interest to those departments and agencies con-

[2] For these and other roots of the NSC, see *ibid.*, 899–901; U. S. Senate, Committee on Naval Affairs, *Unification of the War and Navy Departments and Postwar Organization for National Security, Report* to Hon. James Forrestal, Secretary of the Navy by Ferdinand Eberstadt, 79th Congress, 1st Session, 1945, 47–54 (hereinafter, *Eberstadt Report*); Ernest R. May, "The Development of Political-Military Consultation in the United States," *Political Science Quarterly*, LXX (1955), 161–80.

[3] *Eberstadt Report*, 7.

cerned with national security, and suggest guidelines and courses of action to the President. To ensure the availability of an adequate intelligence basis for these deliberations, the 1947 Act also created a Central Intelligence Agency. This Agency, operating under NSC direction, would coordinate all government intelligence activities concerned with national security, would correlate and evaluate national security intelligence, and would advise and report to the Council on all matters within this field.

The National Security Council, while lacking executive authority or in fact any power other than to offer advice, was really an extension of the presidency. With the chief executive as its chairman, its decisions would become his decisions, and its members, as department heads, would be in a position to see that these decisions were carried out. Under a weak president, this sort of arrangement might tend to diminish or diffuse the powers of the chief executive; but under a strong one it would sharpen the decision-making process and render more efficient the implementation of decisions once made. In the final analysis, the personality and individual desires of each president would determine the role and scope of activity of the National Security Council.

Since the creation of the NSC, three strongly different individuals have occupied the White House. Each regarded the Council in his own way; each used it to satisfy his own needs and intentions. And in each administration, the organization of the NSC and its role in the formulation of national security policy have changed to meet the criteria imposed by the chief executive.[4]

I

President Truman's use of the National Security Council,[5] especially in the three years prior to the outbreak of the Korean

---

[4] The best source for a study of the birth and development of the NSC is the collection of hearings, studies, reports, and recommendations on the national security structure compiled by a group headed by Senator Henry M. Jackson and published as U. S. Senate, Subcommittee on National Policy Machinery of the Committee on Government Operations, *Organizing for National Security*, 3 Volumes (Washington, D. C., 1961). Especially useful is the "Organizational History of the National Security Council," prepared by James S. Lay Jr., and Robert H. Johnson, two long-time staff members of the Council, which appears in Volume II of this collection. Unless otherwise indicated, this article is based on these volumes.

War, reflected his strong concern for the authority, responsibility, and prerogatives of the chief executive. Congress had declared that the NSC would consist of certain officials whose function it would be to "advise the President . . . in matters involving the national security." [6] But Truman, among others, seriously questioned whether Congress had the constitutional power to require the President to seek advice from specific individuals before reaching decisions on certain subjects.[7] Truman also recognized that the wording of the National Security Act might be construed to establish the Council as an imitation of the British Cabinet, with similar powers and responsibilities, and a subsequent diminution of presidential authority.[8] . . .

As a means of emphasizing the advisory role of the NSC, Truman did not regularly attend Council meetings. After presiding at the first session of the Council on September 26, 1947, he sat in on only eleven of the fifty-six other meetings held before the start of the Korean War. In his absence, in conformity with Truman's view that the Secretary of State was the second ranking member of the Council and that the Department of State would play the major role in policy development, Secretary Marshall (and later Acheson) presided. Beginning in August 1949, when the Vice-President was added to the NSC, that officer took the chair in the President's absence.

. . . .

This is not to say that Truman regarded the NSC as unnecessary or undesirable. On the contrary, he viewed it as "a

---

[5] For this section, see also Sidney W. Souers, "Policy Formulation for National Security," *American Political Science Review*, XLIII (1949), 534–43; James S. Lay Jr., "National Security Council's Role in the U. S. Security and Peace Program," *World Affairs*, CXV (1952), 37–39. These and some of the other articles cited below are also reproduced in *Organizing for National Security*, II.

[6] National Security Act of 1947, Sec. 101 (a).

[7] On this point, see Robert Cutler, "The Development of the National Security Council," *Foreign Affairs*, XXXIV (1956), 442–43; Hammond, "The National Security Council," 903. President Truman's views on his relations with the NSC are described in his *Memoirs*, II, *Years of Trial and Hope* (Garden City, N. Y., 1956), 59–60, and the quotations in the following paragraphs are taken from this source.

[8] For a fuller discussion of this question, see Hammond, "The National Security Council," 899–901.

badly needed new facility" in the government. . . . But the Council was only "a place for recommendations to be worked out." . . . Only the President could determine policy and reach decisions, and these were functions he could not delegate to any committee or individual. Even when he sat as chairman of the Council and indicated his agreement with a specific recommendation, this did not become final until the NSC submitted a formal document to the President and secured his written approval. "When the President signs this document, the recommendation then becomes a part of the policy of the government." Here was Truman's understanding of the role of the President, and this firm belief determined his relationship with the National Security Council during the five years that it operated under his direction.

． ． ． ． ． ． ． ． ． ． ． ． ． ．

Reorganization Plan No. 4 of 1949, effective in August of that year, placed the NSC in the Executive Office of the President, where it remains today. This move not only formalized a *de facto* situation, but was dramatic evidence of the position of the Council as an advisory arm of the President rather than as any sort of policy-making "politburo."

． ． ． ． ． ． ． ． ． ． ． ． ．

The NSC staff, a small body of permanent Council employees and officers detailed temporarily from the participating agencies, was headed by a nonpolitical civilian executive secretary appointed by the President. An "anonymous servant of the Council," [9] . . . he carried NSC recommendations to the President, briefed the chief executive daily on NSC and intelligence matters and maintained his NSC files, and served, in effect, as his administrative assistant for national security affairs.

The organization of the NSC staff [10] was flexible and, as the Council developed, changed to meet new needs. In general, during the pre-Korean period, it consisted of three groups. First was the Office of the Executive Secretary and the Secretariat, com-

---

[9] Souers, 587.

[10] In this article, the word "staff" refers to the entire NSC staff organization. The "Staff" and later "Senior Staff" and "Staff Assistants" refer to parts of the "staff."

posed of permanent NSC employees, which performed the necessary basic functions of preparing agenda, circulating papers, and recording actions. Next was the Staff, consisting almost entirely of officials detailed on a full-time basis by departments and agencies represented on the Council, and headed by a coordinator detailed from the State Department who was supported, in turn, by a permanent assistant. This body developed studies and policy recommendations for NSC consideration. The third group consisted of consultants to the executive secretary, the chief policy and operational planners for each Council agency. Thus, the head of the Policy Planning Staff represented the State Department, the Director, Joint Staff, represented the Department of Defense, and so forth.

. . . .

Policy papers developed by the NSC fell into four categories. First and most important were the basic comprehensive statements of overall policy, concerned with a broad range of national security problems and the political, economic, and military strategy to be pursued in meeting them. Next were papers bearing on large geographical areas of the world or specific countries. A third category dealt with functional matters such as mobilization, arms control, atomic energy, and trade policies. The final group of papers covered organizational questions, including NSC organization, the organization of foreign intelligence activities, and internal security organization. All of these documents would theoretically dovetail with each other to "form a basis for a balanced and consistent conduct of foreign, domestic, and military affairs related to our national security." [11]

. . . .

Some papers were submitted to the Council merely for information, others solely as a basis for discussion. Those embodying policy recommendations, however, were forwarded to the President, together with any JCS views, by the executive secretary. The President would then reconcile whatever differences of opinion were still outstanding and, if he agreed, place

---

[11] Souers, 539.

his approval on the "Conclusions" section of the paper. The appropriate departments and agencies, as notified by the executive secretary, would then implement the new policy. President Truman developed the practice of designating one department head, normally the Secretary of State, as coordinator of all implementation, and periodic reports were also required by the Council.

Once the President had signed an NSC paper and directed that it be carried out, a new policy had, to all intents and purposes, been established and put into effect. But this did not necessarily make it policy in practice. What gave it reality was the President's "will and capability to get it executed." [12] This might mean a hard campaign on the part of the chief executive to educate or arouse public opinion, a long and arduous legislative battle, or a host of other problems to be met before the policy could truly take effect.

In addition to the formal development of policy papers, the NSC during this period also met a number of times to discuss current problems of vital importance to national security. On these occasions, the Council convened without the formality of elaborate preparations or preliminary briefings. Some of these discussions, of course, served as the basis for policy papers, but in other cases the NSC was simply an intimate forum where the President's top-level advisers could thrash out questions requiring immediate action. The Berlin crisis and blockade of 1948 is a good example of this. With President Truman in the chair and General Lucius D. Clay, American commander in Germany, present to report, the Council met several times to discuss developments and make recommendations that the President could act on immediately.[13]

By the beginning of the Korean War, two years and nine months after the establishment of the NSC, the Council had become a well-integrated, functioning organization. It had held more than fifty meetings and taken over three hundred "actions" in the form of approvals, recommendations, and other deliberations. But the Council was still a long way from being the type of body that its creators had envisioned, and many problems,

---

[12] Hammond, 'The National Security Council," 907.
[13] Truman, II, 124–29.

both functional and organizational in nature, were becoming evident.

.   .   .   .

In the field of policy-making, as Walter Millis put it, "The effect of NSC is not prominent; NSC no doubt considered the staff papers, debated policy and arrived at recommendations, but every glimpse we have been given of the actual policy-making process in this period shows Defense, State, the Budget Bureau, the White House, making the independent determinations — usually on a hasty if not extemporaneous basis — which really counted." [14] . . .

If this situation was the result of Truman's unwillingness to use the NSC as Eberstadt had envisioned its use, there were other weaknesses in the system, a few reflecting the President's attitude but others probably the standard organizational growing pains to be expected in such a new and completely different agency.

In the first place, attendance at Council meetings, originally limited to the statutory members, had gradually broadened to include the consultants and other departmental advisers. This not only made for too large a group for free discussion, but also encouraged NSC members to look to their departmental advisers and to present their departmental rather than individual views of problems. In the absence of the President, moreover, discussion was more rambling and diffuse than if he had been present, and important actions were sometimes delayed or taken later outside the Council. Then too, while the executive secretary briefed the President on the meeting, Truman could neither hear the direct expression of individual viewpoints nor, more important, could he discuss these with Council members. This sometimes led members to seek out the President after an NSC meeting and give him their ideas separately, a procedure that downgraded even further the relative importance of the Council as a corporate body.

There were also problems in the functioning of the NSC staff. Other agencies that detailed individuals to the Staff tended increasingly to look upon these people as "foreigners," out of

[14] Millis, 223.

touch with problems and attitudes of their parent organizations. The NSC consultants, on the other hand, heavily engaged in responsibilities within their own departments, were less and less able to devote attention to NSC matters. As a result, Council members began to by-pass the Staff, submitting their policy recommendations directly to the Council, and, at the same time, the Council tended to refer many of its problems not to the consultants but rather to *ad hoc* NSC committees. The absence of sound preliminary staff work frequently led to confusion and delay, as did the necessity for relying on *ad hoc* committees, unfamiliar with the overall national security picture and hampered by difficulties of coordination and perspective. An additional problem was the absence of JCS representation on the Staff, which made it hard to anticipate and allow for probable JCS views on papers before they reached the Council table.

And finally there was the growing anomaly of the Staff representative of the State Department holding the position of Staff Coordinator at a time when the bulk of matters coming before the Council was no longer concerned primarily with foreign affairs. ... What was needed, clearly, was a Staff Coordinator without departmental ties and one, moreover, in close and constant contact with the President and thus personally familiar with his views and requirements.

Recognition of all of these problems led, in late 1949 and early 1950, to considerable study of the role and procedures of the NSC. As a result ... a number of functional and structural changes took place.

Within a few days after the beginning of the war in Korea, Truman directed that the NSC would meet regularly each Thursday and that all major national security recommendations would be coordinated through the Council and its staff. He himself began presiding regularly at these sessions, missing only nine out of seventy-one NSC meetings held from June 28, 1950, through the end of his administration in January 1953.

In late July 1950, in a directive again underlining the role of the Council in policy formulation, Truman ordered a reorganization and strengthening of the NSC. He limited attendance at NSC meetings to statutory members [15] plus the Secretary of the Treasury, the Chairman, JCS, the Director, CIA, the Special Assistant to the President (W. Averell Harriman), Sidney W. Souers (former Executive Secretary and at this time a Special Consultant to the President), and the Executive Secretary. No one else would be present without Truman's specific approval. The President also directed a reshuffling of the NSC staff. The permanent Secretariat remained, but the Staff and consultants were replaced by a Senior Staff and Staff Assistants. The Senior Staff was composed of representatives of State, Defense, NSRB, Treasury, JCS, and CIA, and shortly thereafter of Harriman's office, and headed by the Executive Secretary, an official without departmental ties. Members were generally of Assistant Secretary level or higher and in turn designated their Staff Assistants.

.   .   .   .

In the first year after the beginning of the Korean War, the NSC and its Senior Staff were quite active with the Council meeting about three times each month and the Senior Staff getting together at least twice weekly. By the end of 1951, however, the Council was meeting on an average of a little less than twice a month, the Senior Staff about once a week, and NSC activity was generally lighter. For the most part, during the Korean War phase of the Truman administration, the NSC played a somewhat larger role in helping to formulate national policy. Yet as a body it was still not dominant, since the President continued to look to individuals or other agencies for advice and recommendations in the national security field. The NSC "provided a convenient mechanism" for staffing and coordinating interdepartmental views, but "its position was still somewhat casual." [16]

.   .   .   .

II

If Harry S. Truman to a large extent limited the role of the National Security Council in policy formulation and integration,

---

[15] The President, Vice-President, Secretaries of State and Defense, and Chairman, National Security Resources Board.

[16] Millis, 255, 388.

Dwight D. Eisenhower may be said to have institutionalized it. President Eisenhower "reactivated NSC and infused into it a greater responsibility than it had enjoyed under Truman." [17] . . .

During the 1952 election campaign, presidential condidate Eisenhower criticized Truman's use of the NSC. He promised that if elected he would elevate the Council to the position originally planned for it under the National Security Act and use it as his principal arm in formulating policy on military, international, and internal security affairs. Accordingly, he asked Robert Cutler, the Boston banker who was soon to become the new President's Special Assistant for National Security Affairs, to make a study of the NSC and recommend way and means of improving it. Cutler's report, submitted to Eisenhower in mid-March 1953, became the basis of an immediate structural and functional reorganization aimed at systematizing the NSC. Subsequently, these initial changes, and other studies, led to further adjustments during the eight years of the Eisenhower administration.

By 1960, the NSC had developed into a highly complicated but nonetheless smoothly operating machine, with clear lines of authority and responsibility and elaborate yet systematized staff work.[18] The heart of the machine was, of course, the Council itself, with its five statutory members: the President, Vice-President, Secretaries of State and Defense, and Director, Office of Civil and Defense Mobilization.[19] The Council met regularly on Thursday mornings. In addition to the statutory members, as many as a score of others might be present. Normally, the Secretary of the Treasury and the Budget Director attended NSC meetings and, when items pertinent to their responsibilities were being discussed, so did the Attorney General, Chairman, Atomic Energy Commission, and Administrator, National Aeronautics and Space Administration. At the determination of the President,

---

[17] *Ibid.,* 182.

[18] For a step-by-step account of organizational developments, see Lay and Johnson, 23–52.

[19] With the abolition of NSRB in 1953, the Director, ODM, replaced the NSRB chairman on the NSC and in 1958 this NSC membership was assumed by the Director, OCDM. Membership in the NSC of the Director for Mutual Security (subsequently the Director, Foreign Operations Administration) was dropped in 1955.

officials such as the Secretary of Commerce or the Chairman of the Council of Economic Advisers might also be present for specific items. Occasionally private citizens, appointed by the President as informal advisers to the Council, might appear to present and discuss their reports. And a large number of others, not formal participants, also attended regularly in various capacities. The JCS Chairman and CIA Director were there as advisers. The Assistant and Deputy Assistant to the President, the Director, USIA, the Under Secretary of State for Economic Affairs, the Special Assistants to the President for Foreign Economic Policy and for Science and Technology, and the White House staff secretary all attended as observers. Staff representation was provided by the President's Special Assistants for National Security Affairs and for Security Operations Coordination and by the NSC Executive and Deputy Executive Secretaries.

As Chairman of the Council, the President was directly supported by two White House Staff members, the Special Assistants for National Security Affairs and Security Operations Coordination. The former was by far the more important. The principal supervisory officer of the NSC, he advised the President on the Council agenda and briefed him before each meeting, presented matter for consideration at the meetings, appointed (with the President's approval) special committees and consultants, and supervised the executive secretary in the direction of the NSC staff. He also had the major responsibility of chairing the Council's two major subsidiary organizations, the Planning Board and the Operations Coordinating Board.

The NSC Planning Board had essentially the same functions as the old Senior Staff and a similar, somewhat expanded, membership. It met regularly on Tuesday and Friday afternoons. Those agencies with permanent or standing representation on the Council itself were represented on the Planning Board by officials at the assistant secretary level, nominated by the department heads and approved by the President. Advisers from JCS and CIA as well as the Special Presidential Assistant for Security Operations Coordination also attended meetings, as did observers from other interested agencies. Staff representation consisted of the NSC Executive and Deputy Executive Secretary and the Director of the Planning Board Secretariat. Planning

Board activities were supported by a staff of Board Assistants, the old Staff Assistants under a new name.

The second major staff agency of the NSC was the Operations Coordinating Board. . . . The purpose of the . . . OCB was not only to coordinate and integrate psychological with national strategy, but also, and more importantly, to act as the coordinating and integrating arm of the NSC for all aspects of the implementation of national security policy.

The OCB met regularly on Wednesday afternoons at the State Department. Permanent membership included the Under Secretary of State for Political Affairs, Deputy Secretary of Defense, Directors, CIA, USIA, and ICA, and the Special Assistants to the President for National Security Affairs and Security Operations Coordination (who served as Chairman and Vice-Chairman respectively). The Chairman, AEC, Under Secretary of the Treasury, and Deputy Director of the Budget attended on a standing basis and other agencies participated on an *ad hoc* basis. An elaborate staff supported the Board, and several of its members normally attended OCB meetings. Despite the strong military representation in other parts of the NSC, no representatives of the JCS participated in the activities of either the OCB or its staff.

Completing the organizational structure of the NSC were the Interdepartmental Intelligence Conference, the Interdepartmental Committee on Internal Security, and other special and *ad hoc* committees, and the NSC staff, which included the Planning Board, OCB, and Internal Security Coordinating staffs.

President Eisenhower's concept of the NSC, as stated by him, was that

> The Council is a corporate body, composed of individuals advising the President in their own right, rather than as representatives of their respective departments and agencies. Their function should be to seek, with their background of experience, the most statesmanlike solution to the problems of national security, rather than to reach solutions which represent merely a compromise of departmental positions. This same concept is equally applicable to advisory and subordinate groups, such as the Joint Chiefs of Staff, the NSC Planning Board, and the Operations Coordinating Board; although the members of the

latter two Boards are responsible also for stating the views of their respective departments and agencies.[20]

Within this concept, policy formulation followed a somewhat formalized pattern. A subject for consideration or action might be raised by any part of the NSC system, from the President on down. It might deal with a new problem area, the result of some particular development in world events; it might merely be a suggestion that a standing policy be reviewed; it might be a combination of these or other factors. Discussion or preparation of a preliminary staff study would then begin within the Planning Board. A first draft, prepared by the agency of primary interest, would next be considered, gone over by the Board Assistants working with others within their own departments, and then restudied by the entire Board. This procedure might be repeated several times, frequently in smaller subgroups and often in conjunction with outside consultants, and the whole process would constantly be monitored by the Special Assistant for National Security Affairs and the Executive Secretary. Before formal Council consideration, finally, each member would receive an advance copy of the paper, with JCS comments, and be individually briefed by his Planning Board representative.

Under the Eisenhower administration, NSC papers included a Financial Appendix, something they had not previously contained. This document, specifically called for by the President as a regular part of most NSC papers, was intended to indicate the fiscal implications of the proposed policy and was to be carefully considered by the Council in determining its recommendations.

President Eisenhower sometimes made his decision on these recommendations at the NSC meeting itself, but in most cases a formal record of actions was circulated for comment by the members before it was submitted for final presidential approval. Once the President had made his decision, it was the OCB's function to coordinate and integrate the activities of those departments and agencies responsible for executing the new policy.

The OCB had no authority to direct or control these activities,

[20] Quoted in *Organizing for National Security*, II, 129. See also Lay and Johnson, 32–33.

but it provided a means by which the responsible agencies could consult and cooperate with each other. The Board's own operations were limited to advising, expediting, and following up, although since OCB members were on the Under Secretary level they each had enough authority within their own agencies to see that agreements reached within the Board were carried out. Also, while it did not make policy, the OCB developed or initiated new proposals for action within the existing framework of national security policies. In practice, all of the Board's activities were limited to policies affecting international affairs, since other coordinating mechanisms already existed for the fields of internal security and defense mobilization.

.   .   .   .

The neatness and mechanical order of this process was praised by its supporters as the most efficient means of transacting the heavy load of business with which the National Security Council concerned itself under President Eisenhower.... Critics, however, labeled this "mass production, packaging and distribution," and questioned whether truly effective policy could be developed by a form of standardized bulk processing.[21] In reply, supporters of the system pointed out that in times of emergency — President Eisenhower's two illnesses, for example — it had provided a "reservoir of accumulated policy guidance" that enabled agency and department heads to continue functioning with the full knowledge that they were following approved guidelines within "the broad policy concept established by the President."[22]

This sort of exchange was typical of the growing controversy over the NSC that had developed by the late nineteen-fifties. Critics admitted that the Eisenhower NSC had "infused a new order and system into decisions which were once more various and chaotic," that it had "assisted in bringing the departments together in more orderly and cooperative effort" in areas of "comparatively minor importance,"[23] and that its theoretical poten-

---

[21] Millis, 390.

[22] Cutler, 445; Dillon Anderson. "The President and National Security," *Atlantic Monthly*, CXCVII (1956), 46.

[23] Millis, 391. Critics and defenders of the NSC under Eisenhower, especially the former, are amply represented, in *Organizing for National Security*. See also Hammond, "The National Security Council," 903–10.

tialities were great. But they also charged that the Council was incapable of dealing with large, basic problems, that it was over-staffed, excessively rigid, and unable to bring any real focus to bear on major aspects of national security policy.

Basically, they argued, the NSC was a huge committee, and suffered from all the weaknesses of committees. . . . The result, as former Secretary of State Dean Acheson charged, was "agreement by exhaustion," [24] with the ponderous NSC machinery straining mightily to produce not clear-cut analyses of alternate courses, but rather compromise and a carefully staffed "plastering over" of differences.

The Presidential decision, therefore, was based on no deliberate measuring of opposing views against each other, but on a blurred generalization in which the opportunity for choice had been submerged by the desire for compromise. Approved national policy statements, it was argued, were thus not only imprecise, but were also far too broad and sweeping to be applied to specific problems. They were consequently all things to all men, with each protagonist of a different line of action finding justification for his own view in the vague or general wording of an approved paper. Even with the best of intentions, an agency or department head often could not divine the precise meaning of an approved policy with consequent and obvious difficulties in implementing it.[25]

Nor was the OCB of much use in solving the problem. An interdepartmental committee with no authority, it engaged in the same sort of bargaining and negotiation in interpreting and implementing policy as had the Planning Board and Council in creating it. Frequently by-passed or ignored, also, the OCB in

---

[24] Dean Acheson, "Thoughts About Thought in High Places," The *New York Times Magazine*, October 11, 1959, reproduced in *Organizing for National Security*, II, 292. The theme of the legislation of strategy is developed at length in Samuel P. Huntington, *The Common Defense: Strategic Problems in National Politics* (New York, 1961), 146–66.

[25] The implications of this for military commanders and especially for the JCS were explained by former Army Chief of Staff General Maxwell D. Taylor before the Jackson subcommittee and in his own book: *Organizing for National Security*, I, 787–99; Taylor, *The Uncertain Trumpet* (New York, 1960), 82–83 and *passim*.

the final analysis had little effect on the actual coordination of policy execution.

To make matters worse, the critics went on, the NSC system by its very nature was restricted to continuing and developing already established policies and was incapable of originating new ideas and major innovations. Council members were either too busy in their own agencies or too intent on promoting departmental viewpoints to take the free and unfettered approach to their work on the NSC that was necessary to initiate fresh and imaginative policies. NSC members were well aware, also, that much of national security policy was in fact developed and co-ordinated outside of the Council, through the Budget Bureau, the Cabinet, or separate policy groups that dealt with matters like disarmament, manpower and reserve policy, or executive organization, or through individuals like the Secretaries of State or the Treasury who exercised personal influence with the President. Frequently departments or agencies purposely by-passed the NSC system in order to ensure the success of critical proposals. Indeed, the whole question of whether national policy was best developed by an NSC consisting of the officials who would implement this policy, and could thus best understand the attendant problems, or by independent bodies of thinkers not limited by operational restrictions was sharply underlined by President Eisenhower's increasing use of outside committees of private citizens to study important problems in the national security field.

To all of these criticisms, the supporters of the NSC system replied vigorously, either denying the accuracy of the critics' premises or the validity of their conclusions or arguing forcefully that if the Council machinery were less than perfect, it was nevertheless an extremely effective means of developing national security policy and the one best suited to the ideas and methods of President Eisenhower.

Some critics, in disparaging the Eisenhower NSC system, had admitted that the policies it developed would probably have been the policies of the Eisenhower administration in any event. Gordon Gray, Special Assistant to the President for National Security Affairs during most of Eisenhower's second term, implied strong agreement with this view. "I suspect," he said, "that the unhappiness of any knowledgeable person with respect to the NSC and its procedures really derives, not from a concern about how the machinery works, but what it produces. This, then, is substantive disagreement. For those, the only solution would seem to be to elect a different President." [26]

III

In April 1959, Senator Henry M. Jackson, in a memorable address to the students of the National War College and Industrial College of the Armed Forces, vigorously attacked the Eisenhower NSC system. Summing up many of the criticisms already voiced by others, he referred to the Council as it then functioned as "a dangerously misleading façade." He had, he announced, recently proposed a full-scale, nonpartisan congressional study of the whole problem of formulating national security policy with a view to making definite recommendations for "constructive remedies." [27]

Three months later Jackson found himself at the head of a Subcommittee on National Policy Machinery, a subgroup of the Senate Committee on Government Operations newly established to implement his proposal. The Subcommittee's "inquiry" — to use its own term — lasted more than two years, until the fall of 1961. . . .

By the winter of 1960–61, the Jackson subcommittee had advanced far enough in its work to come up with a number of conclusions and recommendations, which it published for the education of the incoming Kennedy administration. These findings and proposals dealt with many areas of the government, from the President on down to the individual private citizen in the national service, but the National Security Council was, of course, of prime concern.

.   .   .   .

---

[26] Gordon Gray, "Role of the National Security Council in the Formulation of National Policy," prepared for delivery to the American Political Science Association, September 1959, in *Organizing for National Security*, II, 189.

[27] Senator Henry M. Jackson, "How Shall We Forge a Strategy for Survival," April 16, 1959, *Organizing for National Security*, II, 266–77.

To establish a National Security Council of true value to the President, "to 'deinstitutionalize' and to 'humanize' the NSC process," the subcommittee made the following recommendations:

(1) The Council should meet only to advise the President or receive his decision on specific major items. "Council meetings and the Council agenda should never become ritualistic."

(2) The Council should offer a clear expression of alternate courses of action and their implications and "not spare the President the necessity of choice."

(3) Council meetings should be "considered gatherings of principals" and restricted to top officials, with staff attendance "tightly controlled." A written record of decisions should be kept.

(4) The Planning Board should be replaced by a group "used mainly to criticize and comment upon policy initiatives developed by the departments or stimulated by the President." This body should not negotiate or secure agency concurrences. More use might be made of "informal working groups" or outside consultants.

(5) "The President must rely mainly upon the Secretary of State for the initial synthesis of the political, military, economic, and other elements which go into the making of a coherent national strategy." The Secretary was "crucial to the successful operation of the Council."

(6) The OCB should be abolished and "responsibility for implementation of policies cutting across departmental lines should, wherever possible, be assigned to a particular department or . . . action officer, possibly assisted by an informal interdepartmental group."

(7) The NSC staff should be reduced and more closely integrated. A small presidential staff, working "outside the system," should closely assist the chief executive by providing information, suggesting "policy initiatives," and "spotting gaps in policy execution."

(8) The membership on the Council of the Chairman, NSRB, subsequently replaced by the Director, OCDM, was intended to provide the NSC with perspectives on the domestic economy and resources. Since OCDM was less concerned with these problems than with civil defense, the statutory membership of its director on the NSC might well be dropped.

(9) Ways and means should be found of better integrating NSC recommendations with budgetary decisions made outside the Council.

IV

The views of the Jackson subcommittee found a ready audience in the new administration that arrived in Washington in January 1961, for in spirit and content they came very close to matching President John F. Kennedy's ideas of the nature and process of presidential decision-making. Within a very short period after taking office, the new chief executive dismantled the elaborate NSC system so carefully built by his predecessor and replaced it with a loose, flexible, fairly pragmatic set of procedures more suited to his own concepts and methods. Gone was the NSC Planning Board with its highly systematized development of papers, gone the formal, crowded, regularly scheduled meetings of the Council, gone the OCB with its elaborate, interdepartmental follow-up on NSC actions. In their place was a new method of decision-making for national security problems, one that seemed to combine the better features of the informal mechanism developed by Truman and the institutionalized system created by Eisenhower.[28]

Of the old NSC system, all that now remains is the statutory membership in the Council itself — the President, Vice-President, Secretaries of State and Defense, and Director, Office of Emergency Planning [29] — and the President's Special Assistant for National Security Affairs who, assisted by a Deputy and the Executive Secretary, runs the small NSC staff. The Director, CIA, and Chairman, JCS, continue as advisers. Other officials participate in Council deliberations as and when directed by the President, but their participation is on a much more informal and *ad hoc* basis than before.

---

[28] This section is based on the testimony of then Budget Director David E. Bell, Defense Secretary Robert S. McNamara, and Secretary of State Dean Rusk before the Jackson subcommittee and on a letter from Kennedy's Special Assistant for National Security Affairs, McGeorge Bundy, to Senator Jackson, reproduced in the published hearings. *Organizing for National Security*, I, 1173–81, 1215–27, 1323–33, 1335–38.

[29] OEP replaced the former OCDM.

Under President Eisenhower, the NSC was a form of super-department placed atop the traditional structure of executive departments and agencies to solve the problems that individual departments were unable to handle. Under Kennedy, the NSC became only one of several means by which problems may be solved. It took its place beside special Cabinet committees, informal groups of officials, and other bodies organized on an *ad hoc* basis to assist and advise in the national security process. Primary emphasis was returned to the regular departments and agencies and their planning and operational staffs. These, reinforced by interdepartmental committees or task forces and close working, and often personal, relationships between the operating officials, bore the heaviest workload in the national security process.

Normally the President assigned the preparation of a study or recommendation to a Cabinet official or one of his top subordinates. This official, in turn, was responsible for obtaining other departmental views and checking and coordinating with other responsible individuals. Sometimes he did this within small, interdepartmental groups, specially created to study the problem, sometimes by arranging for subordinates in each interested agency to develop the matter. Where appropriate, this included close consultation with the Budget Bureau. Fiscal matters were considered during the development of a study and in drawing up recommendations and proposals; papers no longer had separate financial appendices. The completed report included not only the responsible official's own analysis and recommendations for action, but also a full statement of any differing views held by other agencies or individuals. This was true whether the report was prepared by one person or by a special task force.

The final version, presented to President Kennedy at a formal meeting of the NSC or within smaller or larger panel or subcommittee meetings, was then discussed and, if necessary, debated further before the President made his decision. Once the chief executive approved a specific recommendation, the responsible agency or department made a written record of the decision and the head of that agency, or a high-level action officer, was charged with overseeing its implementation. By placing in the same agency or individual — always the agency or official of primary interest — the responsibility for both planning and implementation, Kennedy

deliberately eliminated the distinction between theory and operation that had existed under the Planning Board–OCB balance,
a distinction felt by many to have been unrealistic and impractical.
If the course of action decided upon was so broad that a single
department did not have overriding responsibility, the decision
was written up by the NSC staff and the President himself might
direct its implementation. Presidential decisions, incidentally,
were no longer recorded as part of elaborate position papers, but
stated briefly in National Security Action Memoranda — referred
to by the initiate as NSAM's — which merely indicated the issue
at hand and what Kennedy had decided to do about it.

. . . .

One regular participant in the NSC who is not a statutory
member of the Council but whose position was obviously unique
was the Attorney General. As the President's brother, Robert
Kennedy had the trust and confidence of the chief executive and
ready access to the White House. He participated actively in the
national security process and served on subgroups or panels of
the Council. He also received the reports of the Interdepartmental Intelligence Conference and the Interdepartmental Committee on Internal Security, which hitherto had been responsible
to the Council through the NSC staff.

The Special Assistant to the President for National Security
Affairs, McGeorge Bundy, also played an important role in the
national security process. Not only was he a top presidential
adviser, but as overall director of the NSC staff he participated in
all Council-related activities. He and his assistants had a variety
of responsibilities in addition to their normal secretariat functions. They suggested areas for consideration and the mechanisms
for handling these and other problems; followed studies through
the planning stage and saw that they were properly coordinated,
staffed, and responsive to the needs and desires of the President;
ensured that a written record was made of all decisions, whether
they were reached at formal NSC meetings or at other top conferences; and kept tabs on the implementation of whatever policy
had been adopted. In this work, Bundy and the NSC staff coordinated closely with other parts of the presidential staff and the

Budget Bureau, performed whatever liaison was necessary, and met frequently with the President at regular White House staff meetings.[30]

Formal NSC meetings were held often but irregularly, sometimes as frequently as three times a week and usually at least once every two weeks. In the first half year of the Kennedy administration, for example, the Council met sixteen times. Many matters that had been considered at regular NSC meetings under Eisenhower were now handled in separate meetings of the President with Secretaries Rusk and McNamara or with a single Cabinet officer, or in committees of the NSC that included only some of the statutory members but also several of their top deputies or other government officials, or at meetings below the presidential level. During the height of the Cuban crisis in October 1962, for instance, Kennedy met almost daily with the so-called Executive Committee of the NSC. This committee consisted of the Chief Executive, Secretaries Rusk and McNamara, Treasury Secretary C. Douglas Dillon, Attorney General Kennedy, CIA Director John A. McCone, JCS Chairman General Maxwell D. Taylor, Presidential Assistant Bundy, and the President's Special Counsel, Theodore C. Sorenson. Also in attendance at many of these meetings were Vice-President Johnson, Under Secretary of State George Ball, Deputy Defense Secretary Roswell L. Gilpatrick, Ambassador at Large Llewellyn E. Thompson, UN Ambassador Adlai E. Stevenson, and former Secretary of State Acheson.[31]

The NSC under President Kennedy, it is clear, was thus a flexible organization within the overall national security structure. Used pragmatically and in a variety of ways, it was only one of several tools that Kennedy employed to help him reach decisions on major issues affecting the security of the nation.

---

[30] For an interesting comparison of Bundy with earlier "White House advisers," see Chalmers M. Roberts, "About Mr. Bundy," *Washington Post and Times Herald*, November 3, 1962, A-9. See also Joseph Kraft, "Kennedy's Working Staff," *Harper's*, CCXXV (December 1962), 31–32.

[31] Stewart Alsop and Charles Bartlett, "In Time of Crisis," *Saturday Evening Post*, CCXXXV (December 8, 1962), 15–20; *Washington Post and Times Herald*, November 1, 1962, A-13.

V

"Fundamentally," as Robert Cutler observed in 1956, "the Council is a vehicle for the President to use in accordance with its suitability to his plan for conducting his great office." A "peculiar virtue of the National Security Act is its flexibility . . . each President may use the Council as *he* finds most suitable at a given time."

The history of the NSC under three chief executives amply bears this out. As a means of assisting the President in the difficult task of forming and implementing national security policy, the Council has played a varied role since its inception. Its role under future presidents may be equally changed, but the need for an NSC or for something similar would appear to be self-evident.

Questions

1. What was the original concept of the National Security Council? Has its development changed the basic role that it was designed to perform?
2. Describe the use of the National Security Council by Presidents Truman and Eisenhower. What was their perception of its function?
3. What are policy papers? How are they utilized?
4. Evaluate the role and function of the Senior Staff.
5. Senator Jackson's subcommittee made several recommendations for changing the NSC. Critically evaluate these.
6. "The virtue of the National Security Act is its flexibility." Discuss.

CIA: Clandestine Services in an Open Society*

Harry Howe Ransom

Harry Howe Ransom teaches political science at Vanderbilt University. He has also taught at Harvard, Princeton, Vassar, and Michigan State. Educated at Vanderbilt and Princeton, Mr. Ransom was a Congressional

*From *Can American Democracy Survive the Cold War?* by Harry Howe Ransom. Copyright © 1963 by Harry Howe Ransom. Reprinted by permission of Doubleday & Company, Inc.

Fellow of the American Political Science Association and Research Associate and senior staff member of the Harvard Defense Studies Program. He is the author of *Central Intelligence and National Security.*

I

The Central Intelligence Agency presents a particular paradox among the many stemming from the conflict between security and liberty. At the entrance to the CIA's new headquarters building near Washington is the biblical inscription: "Ye shall know the truth and the truth shall make you free." [1] Were he permitted through the entrance so decorated, a seriously inquiring citizen would, however, soon discover the agency's operating principles:

... the Central Intelligence Agency does not confirm or deny published reports, whether good or bad; never alibis; never explains its organization; never identifies its personnel (except for a few in the top echelons) ; and will not discuss its budget, its methods of operations, or its sources of information. [2]

So the citizen, as far as CIA's managers are concerned, cannot in fact know "the truth" about a very large, expensive, and increasingly important government agency, the directorship of which has been described as "second in importance only to the President." [3]

The existence of a large, secret bureaucracy sometimes pivotally important in making and implementing national policies and strategies raises special problems. At the level of democratic ideals, the problem is the existence of a potential source of invisible government. At the level of representatives of the people

---

[1] CIA's attachment to John 8:32 also reflects the belief of intelligence professionals in the existence of an objective "truth" in world affairs. If "all the facts" are gathered, they seem to assume, then the problems of policy makers are virtually self-solving. They share this myth with many policy makers.

[2] From mimeographed pamphlet, "The Central Intelligence Agency," issued on request by CIA, Spring 1961, p. 7. Existence of the pamphlet itself seems inconsistent with the secrecy policy declared therein.

[3] Senator Richard B. Russell, Chairman, Committee on Armed Services, in that committee's *Hearing*, "Nomination of McCone . . . ," January 18, 1962, p. 30.

— Executive and Legislative — the problem is primarily how to control a dimly seen instrument, so hot that if not handled with great skill it can burn its user instead of its adversary. The problem for the scholar is access to verifiable information for objective analysis.

The secrecy officially proclaimed by the CIA and affiliated intelligence agencies, and required by the statutes establishing them, quite obviously has not been absolutely maintained. America's open society, particularly the separation of governmental powers, the pluralism of the administrative bureaucracy, and a free press, have made complete secrecy impossible. Journalists and scholars have been able to produce a considerable amount of literature, much of it speculative.[4] The volume has increased as a result of a series of misfortunes or misadventures in recent years, particularly the U-2 incident, the defection to Moscow of two National Security Agency employees, and the abortive attempt to invade Cuba in 1961. These events removed, temporarily at least, the cloak of secrecy to an unprecedented degree. Even with these disclosures, however, our view remains a partial one. One simply cannot apply the usual rigorous standards of data gathering and documentation to this subject. But within limitations, one can analyze some of the dilemmas presented by the existence of a secret intelligence apparatus in a democratic society.

.   .   .   .

---

[4] Relevant scholarly works include: George S. Pettee, *The Future of American Secret Intelligence*, Washington, D.C., Infantry Journal Press, 1946; Sherman Kent, *Strategic Intelligence for American World Policy*, Princeton University Press, 1949; Roger Hilsman, *Strategic Intelligence and National Decisions*, Glencoe, The Free Press, 1956; Washington Platt, *Strategic Intelligence Production: Basic Principles*, New York, Praeger, 1957; Ransom, *Central Intelligence and National Security;* William M. McGovern, *Strategic Intelligence and the Shape of Tomorrow*, Chicago, Regnery, 1961; and Wohlstetter, *Pearl Harbor*.

Important journalistic accounts are: Tully, *CIA, The Inside Story;* Sanche de Gramont, *The Secret War*, New York, Putnam, 1962; Karl E. Meyer and Tad Szulc, *The Cuban Invasion*, New York, Praeger, 1962; David Wise and Thomas B. Ross, *The U-2 Affair*, New York, Random House, 1962; and William L. White, *The Little Toy Dog*, New York, Dutton, 1962.

The list of periodical sources, mostly journalistic, is longer. Notable is Allen W. Dulles, "The Craft of Intelligence," *Harper's Magazine*, April 1963, pp. 127–74, to be published later in expanded book form.

In gathering information, Intelligence [5] must have the objectivity and detachment from policy that will assure the most forthright possible reporting on world affairs But this detachment should not be such that Intelligence either develops its own policy preferences or loses contact with the informational needs of the policy makers. Its duty is to report objective facts without regard to whether they spell good or bad news for existing policy preferences, but with appropriate regard for policy alternatives. In its operational (political warfare or overseas counterintelligence) missions Intelligence must serve always as an instrument of foreign policy and never be allowed to make its own policy.

Knowledge, however, conveys power. Secret knowledge can become secret power. A secret intelligence apparatus, claiming superior knowledge from undisclosed sources, and operating — because of legitimate secrecy claims — outside the normal check-reins of the American governmental system can wield invisible power either in the policy-making process or in clandestine operations in other countries.

. . . .

II

A policy maker must contend with three major considerations in reaching a decision: First, what are the policy objectives or goals being sought and what are the risks or probable costs in seeking them, in terms of alternative values that might have to be sacrificed? In other words, if a certain value is placed on military security as an òbjective, must other policy objectives, such as self-determination and economic development, be sacrificed in some calculable degree? Second, what are the pressures and forces likely to shape world affairs whatever course of action is adopted? Put another way, what are the calculable facts and the most probable trends in world affairs? Third, how may one assess the potentialities and limitations of the alternative instruments by which the environment may be influenced in the most favored

---

[5] Intelligence with a capital "I" will be used here to denote the system; lower case "intelligence" will denote the informational "product."

direction? In other words, with national objectives and world trends in mind, how can we best go about attaining our ends?

Traditionally, the intelligence services are concerned only with the second of these and not with national values, ends, or means. Yet all are inextricably entwined. . . . An agency charged with supplying secret information about the state of affairs in the Soviet Union can be a source of great influence in the policy process. To assume that the U.S.S.R. is "mellowing" in its objectives calls for one American foreign policy; to decide that she intends to conquer the world soon, either by surprise attack or otherwise, for quite another.

There are, to be sure, checks on the growing influence of secret intelligence. In the American governmental system, long-range policies or major shifts in existing policy are determined normally only after an elaborate consensus-building effort. An intelligence estimate, no matter what its assumed degree of accuracy, cannot alone determine major policy outcomes. Yet the rapidly changing, increasingly complex nature of world politics seems to be leading to more and more Intelligence participation in national decisions. The senior intelligence professionals in the interdepartmental policy planning units, though in theory they "advise" and do not "recommend," have already come to have great influence. And since intelligence professionals are usually more permanent members of the advisory and policy planning units than are representatives from the State Department or the armed services, who are constantly "rotated" through such assignments, their prestige increases all the more.

. . . .

The ultimate power and the ultimate restraint of democratic government is an informed electorate. While it would make no sense to publish information about legitimately secret intelligence operations, the principle must be maintained that the citizen, or at least his representatives, be as completely informed as possible. A corollary requirement is that the citizen know something about the source and process by which intelligence is produced. There ought to be public confidence in the professional competence of the intelligence services, but in recent years this has been badly shattered.

III

The product generated by the vast machinery of the loosely confederated intelligence community [6] described in the preceding chapter is distributed according to a governmental "need to know" concept. With a few exceptions, neither the product nor the system's organization, functions, and costs are matters of authenticated public record. The rationale for secrecy is that intelligence activities are particularly sensitive in three respects: First, sources of certain types of data would immediately "dry up" if disclosed. Second, espionage and other illegal forms of information gathering should not be officially acknowledged as a government function. In the intelligence tradition, governments always strive to be in a position to "plausibly disavow" espionage. Acknowledgment by top United States officials, in May 1960, of U-2 espionage flights over Russia sharply violated this precedent. Third, underground political actions, which since 1947 have been within the jurisdiction of the CIA, must be secret.

Inevitably and perhaps logically, the Executive branch monopolizes the control of information on all these activities, and within the Executive, the intelligence community has its own inner-circle monopoly. This inner circle can dole out intelligence reports or information on clandestine activities to groups or individuals having, in the opinion of the leaders of the intelligence establishment, a need to know. Although intelligence reports and estimates go regularly and routinely to important decision-making units, their flow is tightly controlled. Information on some sources and some activities, it may be assumed, is never communicated beyond a small group. Some very high-ranking government officials, it turns out, did not know of the U-2 flights over Russia.

.   .   .   .

This situation confronts the American system of government with a two-sided problem: How can there be public control over functions that require secrecy; and how can the effective operation of a two-party system of government be assured when control of the Executive branch gives the party in power a po-

---

[6] For further organizational details, see Ransom, *op. cit.*, Chs. IV and V.

tentially exclusive access to essential information in the field of foreign military policy?

. . . .

No longer a secret, as a consequence of "accidents," are the facts that: espionage activities and clandestine political action overseas on a large scale and by every possible means have been an expanding American government function since 1947; under the cover of weather research and in the ostensible employment of a large private aircraft corporation, American CIA operatives spied on the Soviet Union with long-range aerial cameras and other devices between 1956 and 1960; and by means of a large and complex organization comparable in estimated size and cost to the CIA, the National Security Agency has for some years been operating or supervising a massive network for electronic eavesdropping on adversaries and allies as well.

. . . .

It is often asserted that the CIA has its own foreign policy. Little direct evidence can be brought forth to prove this. The more likely situation is that the CIA has moved on its own in a policy vacuum. Standard operating procedure is for the Ambassadors on the spot to be fully cognizant and in control of clandestine operations. It is hoped that this principle is forcefully applied and will always be. "Civilian control" is as important here as in the use of the military instrument for policy aims.

. . . .

IV

The Central Intelligence Agency's operations, like those of the National Security Agency, are financed by annual Congressional appropriations. Until the sensational disclosures of recent years, however, most Congressmen knew little about the nature and functions of either agency. They know even less about the amount of money annually expended.

Congress as a whole has voluntarily walled itself off from detailed information by statutes requiring secrecy at the discretion of the CIA's Director. In establishing the CIA in 1947,

Congress prescribed its organization and functions in general terms, giving the broadest possible definition to "intelligence," in current usage a term covering a number of distinctly different functions. Wide discretion was left to the National Security Council, for which the agency was to work, and to the CIA Director. Congress made the Director responsible for "protecting intelligence sources and methods from unauthorized disclosure."

In the CIA Act of 1949 Congress went even further, exempting the CIA from existing statutes requiring publication or disclosure of "the organization, functions, names, official titles, salaries or numbers of personnel employed by the agency." [7] The Director of the Budget was proscribed from making the usual reports to Congress. The standard procedures regarding the expenditure of public funds were waived, and the Director's personal voucher alone became sufficient for expenditures for purposes of a "confidential, extraordinary or emergency nature."

The Bureau of the Budget has since established special review procedures for the CIA, and most of the CIA's funds are said to be audited in a regular, albeit classified, manner by the General Accounting Office. The unvouchered funds expended at the discretion of the CIA Director, running to tens of millions of dollars annually, are said to be audited also, but by an even more secret process. The CIA must also participate in the annual cycles of rigorous budget "justifications" within the Executive hierarchy.

. . . .

The discovery that the CIA was sponsoring aerial reconnaissance flights deep within the borders of the Soviet Union in the 1956–60 period was as much a shock to almost all Congressmen as it was to the man in the street. But the CIA leaders could cite Congressional statutes as authority for withholding such information.

. . . .

This was not, however, a dark secret to every Congressman. A few were privy to some details. One such privileged member spoke up on the other side of Capitol Hill the next day. Representa-

---

[7] Public Law 110, 81st Congress, 1st Session, June 20, 1949, 63 Stat. 208.

tive Clarence Cannon, a Democratic Congressman since 1923, as Chairman of the House Committee on Appropriations told his colleagues that, although members were unaware of it at the time, they had earlier appropriated money for the U-2 program and other unspecified espionage missions. . . .

To justify the fact that some senior appropriations committee members as well as the more junior Congressmen had been hoodwinked into approving camouflaged appropriations for secret intelligence operations, Representative Cannon cited "absolute and unavoidable military necessity, fundamental national defense." He explained that the privileged subcommittee that knew of and approved the U-2 flights included for the most part the same legislators who were privy to the secrets of the atom bomb in World War II. The U-2 flights were, he said, the CIA's response to insistent Congressional demands that the nation be forewarned of enemy attack. Presumably they were also in response to the Strategic Air Command's demands for better target information to bolster "deterrence." Tight secrecy about such matters was required, Cannon implied, because "some incautious member of a congressional committee or its staff" might disclose highly sensitive information.

Cannon's House appropriations subcommittee is not the only House group concerned with intelligence. A special House Armed Services subcommittee was activated in 1958 by Chairman Carl Vinson, Democrat, Georgia, amidst Capitol Hill discontent with intelligence performances. This committee is composed of four members of the majority party, three from the minority, and reviews CIA activities, according to its spokesman, "to the fullest extent it deems necessary." [8]

A similar group exists in the Senate. The Senate Armed Services Committee has, since 1955, maintained a formal subcommittee on Central Intelligence composed of five of its highest ranking members of both parties, all of whom are also senior members of the Senate Committee on Appropriations. This subcommittee receives "information on the magnitude of the CIA appropriation and the purposes for which this money is spent."

---

[8] Letter to author from Chief Counsel, House Committee on Armed Services, October 7, 1960.

Its chairman, Senator Richard B. Russell, Democrat, Georgia, said in 1960 that the CIA was "very cooperative," and that he "knew in advance of the U-2 aircraft and its capability." [9] The group, like the others concerned with the CIA, holds its meetings in secret; no record of subcommittee actions has ever been released.

. . . .

A Hoover Commission task force headed by General Mark W. Clark made a detailed survey of the central intelligence system in 1955 which resulted in two reports. One, dealing with organizational aspects, was published. The other, dealing with secret operations, was top secret. The Clark Task Force made special note of the CIA's freedom from the public surveillance normal to our governmental system. Believing this potentially dangerous, it recommended the establishment of Executive and Congressional watchdogs. The Executive group would be a Presidential board of distinguished private citizens. The Congressional group would be a "Joint Congressional Committee on Foreign Intelligence, similar to the Joint Committee on Atomic Energy."

The Joint Congressional Committee idea was not adopted because of Presidential opposition and a similar coolness among senior legislators. But the first recommendation led to the creation, in February 1956, of the President's Board of Consultants on Foreign Intelligence Activities. Its specified duties were to "conduct an objective review of the foreign intelligence activities of the Government and of the performance of the functions of the Central Intelligence Agency . . . and report its finding to the President semiannually or at more frequent intervals. . . ." [10] The Board's jurisdiction covered not only CIA but all government intelligence agencies. The Director of Central Intelligence was required to reveal to Board members any information demanded, and Board members were sworn to secrecy.

After the 1961 Cuban fiasco President Kennedy reconstituted this Board, changing its name to the President's Foreign Intelligence Advisory Board. On May 2, 1961, James R. Killian was

---

[9] Letter to author, November 3, 1960.
[10] Executive Order 19656, February 6, 1956.

reappointed chairman,[11] a post he once held under Eisenhower.

Concurrently, President Kennedy summoned former Army Chief of Staff, General Maxwell D. Taylor, to make a special study of the Cuban failure and of America's capabilities for paramilitary operations and guerrilla warfare. General Taylor was assisted in this study by Attorney General Robert Kennedy, Chief of Naval Operations Admiral Arleigh Burke, and CIA Director Allen Dulles. The aftermath was a delayed but major shake-up in the top leadership of the CIA. Within a year after the Cuban affair, the Director and Deputy Director had retired and were replaced by John A. McCone, former shipbuilder, Air Force official and Chairman of the Atomic Energy Commission, and Major General Marshall S. Carter, a career Army officer. Functional deputy directors for "plans" (secret operations) and "intelligence production" were also replaced within the year. But major organizational changes, as of this writing, have not been disclosed.[12]

One point to note about surveillance is that the Executive has not usurped monopolistic control of the CIA. Rather, Congress voluntarily, by statute, gave the President and the National Security Council wide and undefined discretionary authority. Only a few specific statutory restraints were placed on the agency: that it have no policy or internal security functions; that it not foreclose or usurp the foreign intelligence work of existing departments and agencies; and that it be given access to FBI files only upon written request from the CIA Director to the FBI Director.

---

[11] New members added included Robert D. Murphy, veteran State Department official; Professor William L. Langer of Harvard, former OSS, State Department, and CIA official; Clark Clifford, a White House adviser to Presidents Truman and Kennedy; and Frank Pace, of broad industrial and government experience. Clifford succeeded Killian as chairman in May 1963.

[12] While there was much speculation, after Cuba, about reconstituting CIA as an exclusively information-gathering agency, assigning clandestine political and paramilitary missions elsewhere, such radical surgery apparently has not been performed as of the end of 1962. For a provocative discussion of possible changes, see *The New Republic*, June 19, 26 and July 3, 1961.

V

Who determines specific policies and operating programs for the Central Intelligence Agency? Because the CIA is but a central unit among various overlapping, duplicating, and inevitably competing intelligence agencies, who arbitrates the jurisdictional disputes? The working constitution of the intelligence system is a set of National Security Council Intelligence Directives, stemming from Congressional statutes of 1947 and 1949. While such directives bear the imprimatur of the NSC, this may be little more than "rubber stamp" approval of working rules and jurisdictional assignments made under the leadership of the Director of Central Intelligence among the various cooperating (or competing) units of the intelligence community. These directives, codified in 1959, set forth the operational and organizational principles of the CIA and assign functions among the various other intelligence units of government. From these basic NSC directives, Director of Central Intelligence directives are formulated to guide the operations of the agency and to coordinate government-wide foreign intelligence activity, in the hope of preventing duplication or gaps in essential information.

The "public interest," then, is represented by the President, advised by the NSC; a handful of senior legislators on Capitol Hill; and the President's Foreign Intelligence Advisory Board. The latter group is not statutory and serves, on a very part-time basis, at Presidential discretion. The question remains: Is this system for surveillance adequate, given the scope and importance of the intelligence function and the potentially explosive nature of some types of operations that have come under the rubric of "intelligence"?

. . . .

... It is my own belief that the system would benefit rather than suffer from additional external surveillance, because of the inherent value within a government bureaucracy of the feeling of external responsibility and the fear of being embarrassed or called to account.

Perhaps 80 to 90 per cent of the activities of the Intelligence Community could be scrutinized by a Joint Congressional Committee to the same degree that existing committees oversee the defense establishment, foreign affairs, and atomic energy policies and programs. These fields too contain highly sensitive elements from a security viewpoint. The record of Congress in keeping secrets given to its various committees in "executive" (secret) session is good. Probably more secrets have deliberately "leaked" from the Executive branch than from Congress.

. . . .

In her search for democracy America produced a government system that fragments and diffuses power. To recommend giving Congress a more institutionalized role in overseeing central intelligence is not to recommend more diffusion of power but less. A Joint Congressional Committee on Central Intelligence would be a center of countervailing power, and should help to focus responsibility and authority.

There is also the troublesome question of whether meaningful debate can occur, particularly in national elections, when sometimes crucial information is in the control of the party in power. During the 1952 election campaign, President Truman established the precedent that the Presidential and Vice Presidential nominees of both parties receive foreign intelligence briefings from the Central Intelligence Agency. His purpose was to assure foreign policy continuity, regardless of the condidate elected. Since such information is highly classified, however, it may be used for background purposes only, and this limits debate on decisive issues. Aware of this, General Eisenhower, in accepting Truman's offer, did so with the understanding that, except for security information, it would "in no other way limit my freedom to discuss or analyze foreign programs as my judgment dictates." . . .[13]

VI

The foregoing analysis suggests some guidelines that may be useful in assuring that the intelligence services are as efficient as possible and under the control of responsible authority. Opera-

---

[13] *The New York Times*, August 15, 1952.

tional intelligence activities must, above all, never be more or less than instruments of national policy, and even as such should not be overrated. Some missions are better left to diplomats. In their informational function, intelligence services must preserve their objectivity. At the same time, Intelligence must serve policy in a staff role rather than attempt to persuade decision makers, openly or subtly, on particular courses of action. And there must be mutual understanding and a close working relationship between the policy makers and the intelligence professionals.

While the control of Intelligence must remain primarily the President's responsibility, Congress must assume a more active and clearly defined role, and the Department of State must participate aggressively in weighing gain from success against cost of failure in every proposed major secret operation. A strengthened Department of State is a prerequisite to putting Intelligence in its proper place.

The CIA is misnamed. More than an intelligence service, it has become a multipurpose organization, engaged in a number of disparate "strategic services." The informational mission of the intelligence system should be organized separately from the clandestine political mission. For when operational planners also supply the ultimate decision maker with the information required to justify a plan's feasibility, great risks abound, with the self-fulfilling prophecy perhaps the most common danger. Planners and operational commanders are notoriously prone to view their proposed plan as an end in itself. As experiences in the Korean War, Laos, and Cuba demonstrate, selecting only those bits of "intelligence" that justify a given plan's practicability courts disaster.

Another problem involves secrecy and the frequent "leaks" that have occurred in this country. Certain strategic services by definition require the utmost secrecy. The United States can impose a higher degree of legitimate secrecy in two ways. First, the leadership of the intelligence community must resist the many temptations to mount the public speech-making rostrum. Wisdom suggests that they cultivate a passion for anonymity.[14] Second,

---

[14] In 1960–61, Allen Dulles, in evidence of his role as a public figure, received the following awards: St. George Association, Golden Rule Award; Veterans of Foreign Wars, Bernard Baruch Gold Medal; All-American

a restoration of confidence in the professional quality of the intelligence system and in the *fact* of its unquestioned subordination to responsible political authority will automatically produce greater self-restraint on the part of Congress and the press.

Perhaps the most fundamental problem, reflected in the apparent bungling in recent times of supposedly secret operations, has been the lack of a clearly defined national purpose and a national consensus on American foreign policy objectives. A clarified national purpose is the most commonly recommended nostrum for the nation's ailments in foreign affairs. Intelligence has borne the brunt of criticism for many policy and operational failures. The blame ought to be shared with the Presidency, State Department, and Congress. Many of the problems of the intelligence system would be self-solving, given a positive consensus on foreign policy aims other than the natural concern for self-survival. In this regard the Communists have an advantage in conducting clandestine political action, for a democracy cannot enforce an ideological dogma. However, dogma places totalitarian regimes at a disadvantage — witness Nazi Germany and now Soviet Russia — because intelligence reports processed through an ideological filter are likely to be inaccurate and misleading. Even with vast intelligence services, Stalin refused to believe that Hitler was about to attack Russia in June 1941; Hitler in his later years habitually refused to hear "bad" news from his intelligence services; and more recently Khrushchev has misapprehended the United States. All leadership suffers from this malady; totalitarians perhaps to the greatest degree.

Some Americans argue that we must refrain from clandestine illegal operations overseas, adhering instead to high moral principles of conduct. While diplomacy is preferable, and usually more reliable and effective than subversion, the United States cannot realistically abstain from espionage or follow an absolute principle

---

Conference to Combat Communism, Vigilant Patriot Award for 1960; New York Employing Printers Association, Franklin Award; and American Committee for the Independence of Armenia, Freedom Award. To his credit, and probably on White House instruction, the new Director of CIA John McCone, through 1962 demonstrated a passion for anonymity as far as public statements are concerned.

of non-intervention in the internal affairs of other nations.[15] Cold War is by definition a stage in international politics that is neither war nor peace. In this situation, and short of a reign of international law based upon the consent of the governed, the United States may sometimes have to engage in clandestine activities to protect the national interest. The nation cannot accept the claim, in every situation, that the existing government or regime in every foreign country is the legitimate one. The national interest and the common defense may require intervention, even though this confronts us with legal and moral problems. The United States rarely faces comfortable alternative choices in support of foreign regimes. Often we must accept the lesser evil because circumstances fail to provide an ideal option.

America can neither unilaterally resign from the Cold War without unacceptable risk to all nations sharing democratic ideals, nor cynically adopt an "ends justify means" rule for action. Intervention or espionage should occur only when no alternative exists, and should be undertaken with a precision and a purpose, determined always by responsible, identifiable political leaders, that have been lacking in the past.

Questions

1. Critics have argued that the function of the Central Intelligence Agency should be limited to information gathering, that the CIA should not be the advocate of specific policies. Do you agree?
2. What might be the advantages of having a secret intelligence service? What might be the dangers?
3. The CIA budget is hidden in various appropriations for other government agencies. Since Congress has responsibility for the budget, should it have knowledge of the way in which the taxpayer's money is spent? This, of course, would involve disclosure which Senator Henry M. Jackson has said, "may be unwittingly giving aid and comfort to the enemy." What is your view?

---

[15] For a good discussion of the problems of intervention in foreign internal politics, see H. Bradford Westerfield, *The Instruments of America's Foreign Policy*, New York, Crowell, 1963, pp. 401–91. For a sketchy treatment see Harry Howe Ransom, "Secret Mission in An Open Society," *The New York Times Magazine*, May 21, 1961, pp. 20, 77–79.